Negotiation Skills
In A Week

Peter Fleming is a Chartered Fellow of both the Chartered Institute of Marketing and also the Chartered Institute of Personnel Development – having been awarded an Oxford Master's in Human Resource Management. With significant retail experience in the UK (marketing and buying) and people development with a UK government agency, he established his own business consultancy group which provides structured learning projects in the UK, Europe and the Middle East.

This is one of several books he has published on negotiation with John Murray Learning, including the follow-up to this title, *Advanced Negotiation Skills In A Week* (2016), and *The Negotiation Coach* (2015), the latter of which applies proven development techniques resulting from his pioneering research on improving the effectiveness of management learning.

Teach Yourself®

Negotiation Skills In A Week

Peter Fleming

First published in Great Britain in 1996 by Hodder & Stoughton. An Hachette UK company.

This revised, updated edition published in 2016 by John Murray Learning

Copyright © Peter Fleming 1996, 1998, 2003, 2012, 2016

British Library Cataloguing in Publication Data: a catalogue record for this title is available from the British Library.

Library of Congress Catalog Card Number: on file.

Paperback ISBN 978 1 473 60961 7

Ebook ISBN 978 1 444 15896 0

1

The publisher has used its best endeavours to ensure that any website addresses referred to in this book are correct and active at the time of going to press. However, the publisher and the author have no responsibility for the websites and can make no guarantee that a site will remain live or that the content will remain relevant, decent or appropriate.

The publisher has made every effort to mark as such all words which it believes to be trademarks. The publisher should also like to make it clear that the presence of a word in the book, whether marked or unmarked, in no way affects its legal status as a trademark.

Every reasonable effort has been made by the publisher to trace the copyright holders of material in this book. Any errors or omissions should be notified in writing to the publisher, who will endeavour to rectify the situation for any reprints and future editions.

Typeset by Cenveo® Publisher Services.

Printed and bound in Great Britain by CPI Group (UK) Ltd., Croydon, CR0 4YY.

John Murray Learning policy is to use papers that are natural, renewable and recyclable products and made from wood grown in sustainable forests. The logging and manufacturing processes are expected to conform to the environmental regulations of the country of origin.

John Murray Learning
Carmelite House
50 Victoria Embankment
London EC4Y 0DZ
www.hodder.co.uk

Contents

Introduction

There was a time, not that long ago, when negotiation was seen, in the main, as the province of industrial relations folk and car-sales advisers. But, no longer!

Repeated financial crises have squeezed profit margins and, in some markets, discouraged buyers from making marginal purchases or continuing habitual expenditure. Managers have found themselves in the frontline of the expectation to achieve better value for money, and the starting point for this is to shop around and explore the offers made by new suppliers, and/or to negotiate better deals with existing suppliers.

Even if your job doesn't involve negotiation, then you might still be an active negotiator when replacing your car, moving house or even selling last season's wardrobe!

The truth is that being a good negotiator has become a life skill, enabling those who are good at it not just to save money, but also to upgrade their computer, television or lawnmower with little or no increase in outgoings – and enhancing their reputation in the process.

Becoming an effective negotiator is certainly within the scope of the majority of people. At its simplest, it involves thinking out what you want, planning how you'd like to get it and developing your powers of persuasion to convince other people that you are simply being reasonable.

So, how do top negotiators achieve their top results?

Well, the starting point is to eradicate some 'no-no's' that could provide obstacles to an agreement. One such no-no is agreeing to meet on the 'opponent's' territory rather than making them travel to yours (where they will feel less comfortable and relaxed and are likely, therefore, to be at a disadvantage). This might just generate additional worries for your opponent, but could also result in aggressive behaviours or even sheer obstinacy ('If that's your game, I'll be blowed if I'm going to co-operate with it').

Then there's the win/lose style (another no-no), which gives no allowances or benefits to the other party – for example, setting extreme demands and becoming confrontational in defence of them. These experiences can sound odd ('Do people really behave like that?' you might say), but when they are under pressure, people can behave in unpredictable ways!

This In A Week publication will help you to plan to become a better negotiator through:

- being better prepared for meetings
- planning clear and realistic objectives for a negotiation
- maintaining concentration
- making logical proposals that create agreement in the other party.

None of this requires a move towards the 'dark arts' or using dishonest strategies – the best negotiators often turn out to be quite ordinary folk who are committed to gaining better results. Congratulations on buying this book, which – if you put its advice into practice – could help you become one of those 'best negotiators'!

Prologue

Our attitude to negotiation is critical because it can make a substantial difference to how we see:

- the solution
- our 'opponents'
- the outcome we would like to achieve.

'Super deals' sometimes make the newspaper headlines, but so, too, do disasters:

UNIONS FLEX MUSCLES AS BOSSES PLAN NEW PAY ROUND

MULTINATIONAL PUTS SMALL SUPPLIER OUT OF BUSINESS

SUPER SALESMAN SELLS 'DUD' CHEMICALS

Many people's reaction to such headlines is: 'If that is what it takes to be a negotiator, you can count me out!'

The fact is that every day many millions of deals are struck which do not lead to strikes, breaches of contract, legal actions, divorces or suicides!

There is always a possibility, though, that something could go wrong – and it is wise to ask yourself about this before setting up a negotiating meeting.

It is important to remember that negotiating may not be essential (or even desirable) in every situation. Alternative approaches or outcomes could include:

- **acceptance** by the other party
- **consultation** of the other party (this could result in erosion of possible objections)
- **selling the idea** (a simple but effective method of persuasion)
- **imposition** (not nice – but sometimes necessary in a crisis situation)
- **arbitration** by another, mutually acceptable and appointed, party (the result is usually binding)
- **mediation** through a neutral third party (who provides an additional communication channel)
- **alternative dispute resolution** – which is useful when all else fails and the parties want to avoid recourse to the law.

SUNDAY

Creating the right environment

You will be more likely to be successful if you know how to create the right environment for negotiation to take place.

Before setting out on a negotiation strategy, it is important to review your motivations for wanting to negotiate in the first place.

Did you identify strongly with the ideas expressed in the 'Prologue' and now want to put them into practice? Or, maybe, you are planning a new 'attack' on your department's objectives (cost controls, sales revenues or even reorganizing work routines) and you fear that there might be some negative reactions.

Today will help you to set up the best environment for a negotiation, so that you avoid distractions and negative factors that can reduce the chances of a successful outcome. This includes:

- reviewing your own attitudes to a negotiation
- creating the best atmosphere for the meeting
- selecting the best time
- selecting the best place.

SUNDAY
MONDAY
TUESDAY
WEDNESDAY
THURSDAY
FRIDAY
SATURDAY

Reviewing your own attitudes

Let's look at an example. Your manager has told you to cut back your team's hours, and the best way to do this would be to make someone redundant. You are concerned that this will cause negative attitudes or even conflict among your team, making you feel that you have to be more insistent and take a more hard-line attitude. This, in turn, might make change more difficult and result in a bad working atmosphere.

Alternatively, you could take a softer, more consultative line, which might bring constructive ideas from the team and engender a better atmosphere. It may even lead, for example, to everyone agreeing to a cut in their hours to 'save' their colleague.

Creating the right atmosphere

Experienced negotiators recognize that there are four possible outcomes to a negotiation:

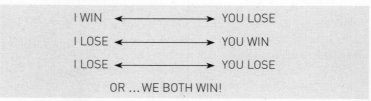

I WIN	⟷	YOU LOSE
I LOSE	⟷	YOU WIN
I LOSE	⟷	YOU LOSE
	OR ... WE BOTH WIN!	

Most people would prefer not to be losers – unless they have unusual motives – and the risk of 'losing' divides negotiators into three categories – those who are:

- **competitive** and want to win at everything
- **collaborative** and want to achieve the best deal for both or all parties
- **consensual** and want to put the importance of maintaining good relationships above any issues which could threaten to divide the parties.

If your role or aim is the continuing development of your business, goodwill or relationships, the collaborative style will bring better, long-lasting relationships and results.

SUNDAY
MONDAY
TUESDAY
WEDNESDAY
THURSDAY
FRIDAY
SATURDAY

So, the right atmosphere will be affected by:

- how you feel about the situation
- how you feel about your 'opponent'
- the relative power of the two parties
- your ability to cope with stressful situations
- your composure – especially with emotional pressure
- how much you trust each other
- your degree of open-mindedness
- your aspirations (Are you the sort of person who would wish to achieve better-than-average results?)
- how prepared you are to listen (as well as to speak)
- your charisma.

Incidentally, our use of the word 'opponent' does not mean 'pistols at dawn'! It is simply a shorthand word to describe the person with whom we are negotiating.

 Remember that, if you want to achieve a win/win deal, your opponent needs to want to arrive at a satisfactory agreement, too. You can influence this by the way you use the ten factors listed above.

Choosing the right time

The 'right time' to negotiate is probably when you have least need for a deal and your opponent's need is greater. However, collaborative negotiators minimize the 'fallout' from such relationships. Otherwise, the opponent may feel 'beaten' and determined to beat you next time. Warfare of this kind can go on for years!

Skilled negotiators:

- choose their timing carefully (avoid the 'bull-in-a-china-shop' approach)
- patiently draw reluctant opponents to the negotiating table (it could take time)
- avoid spontaneous negotiation sessions (if at all possible!)
- prepare their case carefully
- weigh up what they think may be on their opponent's agenda
- know their own limitations and those of their opponents (for example, are you 'sharper' in the mornings or in the evenings?).

Selecting the best place

The right place to negotiate is any place where you feel most comfortable and, as important, most confident.

This comfort factor involves more than just feeling at home. There may be times when your 'home territory' could provide you with disadvantages as well as advantages.

For example, you would prefer not to:

- be distracted by minor queries while trying to concentrate on the negotiation
- be interrupted by telephone calls
- allow your opponents to see the state of your workplace if it is chaotic or somewhat luxurious in their eyes (this might not impress them!).

These factors may help to heighten your opponent's confidence and lower yours. On the other hand, witnessing these things on your opponent's home ground may help you.

Meeting in neutral territory is often suggested by negotiators as an appropriate way of avoiding any bias in the meeting.

However, you should beware of:

- neutral territory which subsequently turns out to be your opponent's home ground
- being 'landed' in a situation in which you do not feel comfortable.

Social situations can put some negotiators at a disadvantage, for example being invited to a more upmarket restaurant than they might have visited previously for a business negotiation – or vice versa!

Perhaps having to work in very cramped conditions, or with bold furnishings, might unsettle some people.

Summary

So, let's summarize our progress today. You should think carefully about how to build a partnership with your opponent.

Look inside your heart and ask yourself:

- Am I really seeking a win/win outcome?
- When will be the best time to negotiate?
- Are we / is our opponent in a hurry?
- How can we use time to our mutual benefit?
- What advantages are there in going to the other party to negotiate or in asking them to come to us?

These questions may seem obvious, but the art of negotiating lies in applying them to your own situation.
Try to relate them to a current project or need. For example, you may be thinking of changing your car. Which of these points might be of greatest help to you today?

Atmosphere	Time	Place

SUNDAY MONDAY TUESDAY WEDNESDAY THURSDAY FRIDAY SATURDAY

Negotiation is not a 'dark art' which should be avoided at all costs! It provides a useful skill that often enables a manager to achieve desirable outcomes with minimal disruption or expenditure.

Setting the scene is a vital part of this process – one which should not be minimized – and tomorrow we will work on more preparations that should contribute to a successful outcome.

Now try our multiple-choice questions to see how you have progressed.

For each question, choose *one preferred answer* (tick the box), then go to the answers at the end of the book to score your choices.

If you chose second (or even third) best answers, then think about why these answers are not as good as our 'top-rated' one(s).

Now turn to the end of the book and make a commitment to your Personal Action Plan.

Progress check (answers at the back)

1. How do you feel when you read of a major negotiation that has achieved an outstanding result?
   a) There must have been some 'fiddling' going on ☐
   b) I'd like to have been around to see it because I bet it wasn't that easy! ☐
   c) If they can do it, I'm sure I should find out more and give it a try ☐
   d) I bet they don't have all the constraints that are put on managers here ☐

2. You have a supplier whose representative is very competitive; their product range is good but you only buy 'necessities' from them as the rep 'winds you up' by trying to make you buy things you don't think you need. Should you:
   a) Continue to keep the rep at a distance and minimize the orders? ☐
   b) Avoid the rep by ordering on line? ☐
   c) Get the problem 'off your chest' and give the rep a piece of your mind? ☐
   d) Politely, but firmly, explain to the rep that you might be prepared to place bigger orders but only on the condition that you will not be pressurized into purchasing items you do not need or want? ☐

3. Where will you have this conversation?
   a) At a local hostelry at the rep's invitation ☐
   b) In your busy office where there are witnesses to record the conversation ☐
   c) In your quiet meeting room where you can both concentrate on making a 'new' start ☐
   d) In a personal letter addressed to the supplier company ☐

4. You experienced bad traffic conditions on the way to work this morning and were an hour late. When you arrived, your assistant told you that your director had called to talk to you about a customer complaint and seemed very cross. Should you:
   a) Call on the phone and try to resolve the problem – starting with an apology for being late? ☐
   b) Go straight to the director's office and try to resolve the problem – starting with an apology for being late? ☐
   c) Ignore the situation and wait for the director to call again? ☐
   d) Delegate your assistant to deal with the problem? ☐

5. You are experiencing a very pressurized work period and are struggling to keep on top of things. You want to take on a new supplier but know little about them, as their base is at the other end of your country. Should you:

a) 'Bite the bullet' by prioritizing the time and task; and learn about the supplier by visiting them before placing the order? ❑

b) Ask for their Annual Report, placing the order if all seems in order and putting off the visit until things are quieter? ❑

c) Ask them for the name of a referee or satisfied customer to gain an independent report? ❑

d) Seek a third-hand report from your (independent) trade body? ❑

6. On your way into work today you noticed that one tyre on your car is almost flat. You had intended to book it into your regular service garage but forgot, and they are 'too busy' to collect it today. You called out an alternative 'emergency service' and the operative has removed the wheel (reporting that the tyre is dangerous) while he prices a replacement. You believe that the quoted price is twice the real cost. Should you:

a) Pay up and put it down to experience? ❑

b) Have a staff member block his vehicle in with the company van, to 'even up the playing field'? ❑

c) Telephone your motoring club to check the normal cost and, if it is lower, tell the operative that that is what you believe the cost should be? ❑

d) Stop taking risks with your own personal safety? ❑

7. You are naturally extrovert, preferring to deal openly with colleagues and team members. One of your team has just been elected by union members as a staff representative and you are worried about and how this development might affect relations in the team. Would you:

a) Warn the individual that you will not tolerate your team relations being 'contaminated' by extremist propaganda? ❑

b) Check how many team members are also members of the union and warn any that are not members not to join? ❑

c) Seek advice from your boss? ❑

d) Welcome your colleague's preparedness to represent their colleagues in meetings/debates and offer your 'counselling support' if it should become necessary? ❑

8. You are visiting a customer in his office and are surprised that all the visitors' chairs are low chairs while the customer has a high adjustable chair. You feel that you would be at a disadvantage sitting on one of the low visitors' chairs.
Would you:

a) Politely refuse to sit down, claiming a bad back and only relenting if your host can provide a higher or high-backed chair? ❑

b) Reluctantly sit down on the low chair and hope that it will not put you at a disadvantage? ❑

c) Explain that this can only be a quick call as you are expected elsewhere, but you'd like to invite the customer to lunch down the road? ❑

d) Leave as soon as it seems polite/decent? ❑

9. Your boss asks you to attend a meeting in the office to agree a cost-saving plan – with a hint that redundancies may result. You are anxious to argue strongly against this but worry that your case will lose impact because of the constant interruptions that are common in the office.
Would you:

a) Refuse to attend unless a quieter venue is found? ❑

b) Book the boardroom, which is quiet and confidential? ❑

c) Hide your doubts and determine to struggle on regardless? ❑

d) Start looking for alternative vacancies in case someone in your team needs them? ❑

10. At the cost-saving meeting your boss accuses you of closing your mind to ways of improving productivity, over-identifying with your team members by defending their interests.
Would you:

a) Seek support and advice from the local union organizer to protect your own position? ❑

b) Present a case for recovery that involves a stronger marketing plan to improve revenue and margins, with milestones for monitoring progress (and with the aim of avoiding impetuous cuts)? ❑

c) Propose a 'no replacement' policy, supposing that individual staff members might decide to chase better opportunities with your competitors? ❑

d) Suggest an in-depth research project of methods used by competitors, which you could then emulate? ❑

MONDAY

Researching your objectives

How do you take decisions? Are you a person who relies on instinct, feelings and emotion, or are you a person who chases down real facts and evidence to support your decisions?

Experienced managers may tell you that they just 'know' the best way to go with a strategy or plan because business goes in cycles and 'what goes around, comes around'! Is this a safe approach? Or should experienced personnel check their facts like anyone else?

Relying on instinct (or even 'luck') may work out well as much as 80 per cent of the time – but is that good enough? Probably not, especially if an incorrect decision could blow a hole in the organization's budget and lead to even more drastic action. And how long do you have to wait before you have enough experience to back 'instinct'?

Managers often find themselves having to take (or influence) decisions that involve deploying resources internally, or committing the organization to external action. In either instance, it is probable that a commitment to the action will be needed from other people – and this may well mean a meeting involving a negotiation (even when there is no buying or selling intention). So, today, we are going to look closer at your negotiation objectives.

Have you ever considered when the worst time for doing the week's food shopping might be? Is it:

- when the store is busiest?
- when stock is running out?
- when you are in a hurry?

If concern about impulse purchasing is uppermost in your mind, the answer has to be:

- when you are hungry!

Of course, you might always prepare a list before starting the shopping expedition – some people do, but many others do not. If you stand and observe your fellow shoppers at the checkout, you can quickly identify those who probably did not bring a shopping list!

There is nothing wrong with buying products we like, but was this a conscious decision or did the final bill come as a shock? The objective shopper starts out with a checklist and then consciously avoids buying any items that are not on the list.

Similarly, the skilled negotiator always prepares a checklist of objectives – a 'shopping list' – and uses it to compare actual results from meetings with those expected. Any move away

from the original plan is then a conscious decision and a target for trading off concessions from the opponent.

Skilled negotiators rarely negotiate without any kind of plan – and most produce detailed plans on anything but the back of an envelope or cigarette packet!

Preparing your own 'shopping list'

Preparing for a dinner party you are going to host may involve some or all of the following:

- deciding on a menu
- preparing a list of ingredients
- making a list of jobs to be done (and by whom)

SUNDAY

MONDAY

TUESDAY

WEDNESDAY

THURSDAY

FRIDAY

SATURDAY

- drawing up a seating plan
- sending out invitations.

Similarly, a decision to move house should lead us to prepare an objective plan. For example, you may have decided to move to a larger house – three-bedroomed, semi-detached with a garage – from your present two-bedroomed terraced house. You will probably start with a 'wish list' for the 'new' house which might read as follows:

- two double bedrooms, one single
- two reception rooms downstairs
- a downstairs cloakroom
- separate garage – close to the house
- gas-fired central heating.

Of course, these items either exist or they do not – but their priority may vary and your view may be very different from that of your partner!

When house hunting we rarely find exactly what we want and this listing will probably provide an important basis for

negotiation at home before you even visit a prospective vendor. The result of these discussions will be a baseline of standards or objectives, against which various possibilities will be screened. You will probably not want to visit properties that do not come up to your expectations (although this is by no means certain – did your present accommodation exactly match your 'minimum' standards?).

Preparing your negotiation brief

Once you have selected a property you find attractive, you will need to produce a negotiating brief for both your purchase and your sale (if you have a property to sell). This will be two-dimensional and encompass:

● your objectives
● your best assessment of your opponent's objectives.

Planning your objectives

Establishing your own objectives will be relatively easy. Taking price as an example, the buyer's objective will be to obtain good value for money bearing in mind the need not to exceed 'market value'. The buyer's parameters for price will be determined by the following:

● At the 'upper end':
  – available funds – from the sale of a current property
  – any bridging finance available
  – a personal loan from your favourite aunt
  – how much you really want the property.

● At the 'lower end':
  – the lowest price you feel the vendor might consider without insulting him/her and causing the withdrawal of the property
  – the price which you feel correctly matches current market activity
  – a price which enables the vendor to meet his/her plans.

Assessing your opponent's objectives

Assessing your opponent's objectives means carrying out some research – at best – and guessing – at worst!

The process requires the ability to put yourself in your opponent's position. For example, a vendor may have chosen to advertise a property at £180,000. It would be surprising (and unusual) if this did not include a 'fall-back position' which would allow for the agent's advice and the fact that some (if not all) potential buyers may make a lower offer.

So, the parameters for the sale may vary between:

(a) Price

Base limit	Ideal position
£ 162,000 ⟵————⟶	£180,000

The 'base limit' here represents 10-per-cent discount on the asking price and could be lower if the vendor is desperate to sell, or if some fault is discovered in the building survey.

(b) Timing

Base limit   Ideal position

5–14 April ←——————————→ 3–31 May

(This would allow for a holiday between 16 and 30 April.)

Of course, there is a lot more at stake when we buy a house, such as how well our own furniture will fit into it and what it will 'feel' like when we are living there. Vendors are often keen to sell items of furnishings such as carpets and curtains and this can be very helpful if the move is a strictly budgeted affair. Expensive mistakes can be made here, too:

(c) Furnishing and fittings

Base limit   Ideal position

Vendor 'gives'   Buyer pays vendor's
contents away ←——————————→ valuation of £10,000
with agreed   for contents
house purchase

As we shall see later, goodwill between buyer and seller may have quite an effect in arriving at the most appropriate point of 'balance' between the two extremes on the three charts. Any breakdown or loss of confidence between the parties can lead to a lose/lose outcome.

Examples of lose/lose results could be:

- either party changing their mind and withdrawing from the transaction (leaving one party, or possibly both, with considerable professional fees to pay – and nothing to show for them)
- carpets and curtains (etc.) put into store rather than being given away (leading to increased costs for the vendor)
- some items 'taken' by the vendor when the buyer expected them to be included in the price (leading to a rearguard action for restitution).

The effect of time

Time can have a crucial effect on the negotiation process, as we shall see later in the week. However, suffice it to say here that a vendor who is being moved by his company (with a tight deadline) may be prepared to consider a lower offer if he is convinced that the contract can be speeded up (e.g. by a cash sale).

Equally, the vendor who is able to put his house contents into storage (bearing in mind his firm's willingness to pay the bill) may be prepared to meet the buyer's timetable, especially when sales activity is depressed.

How do you find out about such levers?

At its simplest, you need to ask:

- friends, family members and so on
- professional advisers (e.g. solicitors, agents)
- people who have moved recently
- your opponent/his family/friends/staff, etc.

OH, NO, HE DIDN'T!!

'My opponent? Surely he or she will not tell you the truth,' you may say. That may be so, but exaggerations or understatements can easily be checked and being 'economical with the truth' may risk the breach of all trust between the parties.

> **TIP** *The broader the issue on which you need to negotiate, the more valuable it is to consult a wide range of people.*

In commercial negotiations the following consulting checklist may prove useful:

- past users of the product/service ☐
- other experienced buyers/sellers ☐
- present referees ☐
- comparison agencies/publications ☐
- advisers ☐
- other people in your own organization (the Japanese use this method to great effect – especially with new business contacts) ☐
- your opponent's own staff. ☐

So, your negotiation brief should include:

- an agenda of issues to discuss ☐
- your objectives expressed in terms of parameters ☐
- questions to ask to reveal information about the negotiation or your opponent's position. ☐

A negotiation brief is not paper for the sake of paper – a systematic approach will pay for itself over and over again!

Pre-meeting planning

The following checklist may help you avoid any loose ends.

Opening

- How should I open the meeting?
- How interested is our opponent in the meeting?
- What needs might exist?
  - Theirs
  - Ours
- What areas of common ground exist between us?

Authority

- Whom am I meeting?
- What is the history/track record of the relationship?
- How much authority does my opponent have?

Power and influence

- What is their 'power' over us and/or our competitors?
- What is our power in this situation?
- How can we exploit our strengths for mutual benefit?

Commitment

- How interested is our opponent in the meeting?
- How badly do they need an agreement?
- Do we want/need agreement today?
- Will a negotiated agreement stick?

Competition/exclusivity

- How might market forces affect the negotiation?
- What leverage might be used?

Innovation and promotion

- What concessions are we likely to have to make to ensure that the deal is successful?
- How innovative are the proposals under discussion?
- Who will contribute what to help?

SUNDAY

MONDAY

TUESDAY

WEDNESDAY

THURSDAY

FRIDAY

SATURDAY

Summary

Researching and planning your objectives (and supporting facts) may not, on their own, produce a convincing argument. However, a negotiation plan – based on a reality that has been carefully and systematically compiled – should give the manager both confidence and a 'winning hand' (especially if your opponent is not as well prepared).

You will still need to prepare to introduce the facts as persuasively as possible, and, even then, you may need a fallback position – especially if your opponent decides to play 'hardball' or is rigidly attached to his/her position. There is a risk of a lose/lose outcome (perhaps no loan agreed, or the probability that your target property will be sold to someone else).

Now that you have worked through Monday's chapter, why not try out your own plans for a car change or a house move or perhaps where you would prefer to spend your summer holidays? The following template could help you with your planning:

SUNDAY

MONDAY

TUESDAY

WEDNESDAY

THURSDAY

FRIDAY

SATURDAY

Your objectives	Opponent's position
1 _____	_____
2 _____	_____
3 _____	_____
4 _____	_____
5 _____	_____

Concessions you can give	**Concessions you seek**
1 _____	_____
2 _____	_____
3 _____	_____
4 _____	_____
5 _____	_____

Questions I need to ask

1 _____

_____

2 _____

_____

3 _____

_____

4 _____

_____

5 _____

_____

Now try our multiple-choice questions to see how you have progressed.

For each question, choose *one preferred answer* (tick the box), then go to the answers at the end of the book to score your choices.

If you chose second (or even third) best answers, then think about why these answers are not as good as our 'top-rated' one.

Now turn to the end of the book and make a commitment to your Personal Action Plan.

SUNDAY

MONDAY

TUESDAY

WEDNESDAY

THURSDAY

FRIDAY

SATURDAY

Progress check (answers at the back)

1. How much importance would you give to the following factors (if you were following the example of high-performance negotiators)?
   a) Your own negotiating position on the current topic ❏
   b) Your opponent's position ❏
   c) The venue for the negotiation ❏
   d) All of the above are equally important ❏

2. If you can choose the time and place for negotiating a 'significant' case, would you choose:
   a) The preferred time/venue of your opponent? ❏
   b) A location by mutual agreement? ❏
   c) Your preferred time/venue (where you believe that you will be on your top form)? ❏
   d) Anywhere and any time – it shouldn't matter! ❏

3. If your opponent's role is to try to agree a wide range of topics/ items with you at the meeting, how should you protect yourself from being tempted away from meeting your own needs?
   a) Be open-minded and prepared to discuss anything ❏
   b) Postpone the meeting until you have a definitive list from the other side ❏
   c) Prepare a definitive list of subjects and your own goals with supporting arguments ❏
   d) Don't do anything ❏

4. Your negotiating brief should concentrate on defining:
   a) Your least favourable positions – every other result would be a 'win' ❏
   b) Some desirable results – taking into account any known outcomes that are defined ❏
   c) Your most favourable position – every other result would be a 'lose' ❏
   d) All of the above ❏

5. Which constraints should be considered when preparing your brief?
   a) Predictions for financial/ trade/world markets ❏
   b) Any likelihood of political pressure ❏
   c) Legal and/or social constraints ❏
   d) All of the above ❏

6. Outcomes of a negotiation are mostly affected by:
   a) How people feel at different times of the day ❏
   b) The amount of effort both parties put into their preparation ❏
   c) When the participants receive their 'pay' ❏
   d) Timing of the economic cycle ❏

7. The suggestion that you could have a (better) offer from your opponent's competitor could be viewed as:
a) An unacceptable insult ❏
b) A powerful tool that always get results ❏
c) A perfectly acceptable 'lever' ❏
d) A one-way tactic which gives the 'user' an edge over the opponent ❏

8. In negotiation, an agenda:
a) Helps to provide a template for the topics for discussion ❏
b) Provides a 'straitjacket' for what would otherwise be an interesting, free discussion ❏
c) Could reduce opportunities for discussing new or additional needs ❏
d) Should be prepared by the boss ❏

9. A concession is:
a) Something you give to make your opponent feel happier ❏
b) A demand you make to 'weaken' the other person's position ❏
c) A factor which you can exchange for a similar concession from your opponent ❏
d) A gift or 'sweetener' to ease agreement ❏

10. Building flexibility into your negotiation brief:
a) Helps ensure that the meeting will not result in a breakdown if either party 'digs in' ❏
b) Gives confidence to both parties ❏
c) Helps the parties explore alternative options leading to agreement around those that are acceptable to both ❏
d) Enables another 'deputy' to take over if one negotiator is unable to conduct the negotiation ❏

TUESDAY

People and places

Have you ever met someone with a 'magnetic' personality – someone who, whatever the situation, seems to carry other people with them?

While this characteristic may not be common, there is no doubt that people who have it can make highly effective negotiators! No matter what the issue or situation, they seem comfortable and persuasive and, most important, engaging.

We may not be able to copy such qualities, but we can develop some of the ways of behaving which can have a similar impact. For example, do you show an interest in others? Are you a good listener, but also someone who has an interesting point of view?

These qualities are valuable if you are planning to persuade other people to agree with you or do something for you – important features of the work of the negotiator.

Salespeople have plenty of opportunities to practise persuading others. The best salespeople are those who have found a natural and acceptable way of selling themselves, which makes selling their product or proposals much easier.

Negotiation is not about having blazing rows with opponents, nor creating an icy atmosphere (although in some circumstances this might prove a useful tactic!). To be successful, negotiators need to be able to persuade other people to agree with them and/or take action, and the successful salesperson undoubtedly has a head start over the rest of us.

Who am I?

Success in negotiation is affected by our ability to demonstrate the following skills and attributes. Rate yourself on this checklist by circling the figure which you feel represents your present skills:

FACTOR	LOW				HIGH	
I am the kind of person who:						
1 presents myself as a person who likes people	1	2	3	4	5	6
2 is positive (Who wants to work with a negative person?)	1	2	3	4	5	6
3 is persistent ('No' can nearly always be turned into 'Maybe' and 'Maybe' into 'Yes')	1	2	3	4	5	6
4 is open-minded (There is always more than one way of achieving an objective)	1	2	3	4	5	6
5 has a good sense of timing and tact	1	2	3	4	5	6
6 has high aspirations for deals (skilled negotiators have high aspiration levels and tend to search for above-average agreements)	1	2	3	4	5	6
7 presents the case assertively (i.e. without waffle)	1	2	3	4	5	6
8 chooses the most persuasive words (use of vocabulary)	1	2	3	4	5	6
9 thinks clearly under stress	1	2	3	4	5	6
10 influences the emotional atmosphere of meetings	1	2	3	4	5	6
11 maintains self-control	1	2	3	4	5	6
12 is decisive	1	2	3	4	5	6

You may not be good at *all* these things but, as this week progresses, awareness may encourage you to experiment ... and practice makes perfect! However, be careful not to experiment in live negotiations which could have a significant effect on your organization's objectives – well, not yet, anyway!

Today's topic is about your personal effectiveness in relations with others and how to identify the strengths and weaknesses of your opponents.

Personal communications and negotiations

One facet of personal effectiveness, when it is applied in negotiations, is the use of an appropriate communications style. There are two specific styles that are used by us all in everyday communication:

- the **extrovert** style
- the **inductive** style.

As may be readily deduced from the names, the first style relates to our attempts to persuade the person to do something by giving them lots of information – in effect, seeking to persuade by 'pushing' your opponent into a position.

The inductive style is concerned with trying to encourage your opponent to do something, by 'pulling' him or her towards that position. Clearly, this approach is more about manipulation and is more subtle than the extrovert style.

The extrovert style

Obvious characteristics of this style are shown below. The person using this style:

- always has a say
- produces lots of ideas and suggestions
- may enjoy a discussion and argument
- quite likes to stir things up in a discussion
- may reveal inner thoughts regardless of the circumstances
- frequently gets his/her own way in conversations.

The style also has a downside which may dilute its effectiveness – especially in extreme cases. If opponents are to be persuaded rather than bludgeoned into submission, these characteristics need to be kept under control. The person may:

- take an aggressive approach to others
- be bluntly honest

- give as good as they get in an argument
- having expressed a point of view sticks to it
- criticize others
- look for all the snags and problems in new ideas.

This style will be most successful, in the short term, when negotiators are working in a powerful situation (i.e. power is on their side) and in a competitive climate. However, if the relationship is dependent on goodwill for its continuing success, there may be a greater likelihood of bruised feelings resulting from the negotiation. This, in turn, may lead to more aggressive tactics being used by the opponent next time (i.e. 'tit for tat').

Characters of the 'old school' who have developed a reputation of being strong negotiators – with a measure of charisma in their personal make-up – may attract a high level of respect from other people. This is particularly noticeable in competitive organizations and in sales-oriented negotiations.

However, the style may not always transfer readily into non-aggressive environments and may lead to the isolation of the negotiator if the style is not appreciated by staff, senior managers, trade unionists or, indeed, customers.

The inductive style

As we have seen, this is the opposite communications style to the extrovert style and, as such, tends to be rather less predictable.

Its relative success is based on the principle that the more you are able to test out the attitudes and arguments of your opponents, the more likely you will be able to pinpoint weaknesses in their arguments. Indeed, the weaknesses may become clearer to them, thus enabling you to induce them to move towards your position.

This style will involve the following conversational skills:

● putting others at ease
● encouraging them to come up with lots of ideas
● being able to extend and develop those ideas
● fostering a warm and friendly atmosphere
● giving credit and praise to others
● taking care to avoid upsetting others.

Do you know people like this? How do you feel about being in discussions with them? Can you imagine your probable response if they were to ask for your help? Most of us would probably be predisposed to help them.

This effect is enhanced further if you are also able to use clarifying behaviour in interactions with others, to ensure that there is a minimum of misunderstandings. This will involve:

- listening carefully to what others say
- checking that you have understood what they have been saying
- finding out what others are saying
- asking lots of open questions (i.e. those that start with 'What', 'When', 'Who', 'Why', 'Where' and 'How').

Your effectiveness will be further enhanced if you are the sort of person who:

- admits to mistakes readily
- conciliates when things get heated
- admits to your weaknesses.

Finally, these skills should enable you to:

- obtain the information from others which you need in any negotiation situation.

The inductive style demonstrates the advantages of co-operating rather than competing with others.

Choosing a style

There is no perfect style that will work in every situation. Both styles have advantages – for example, a sales representative will need to be reasonably extrovert to survive the various 'knocks' from clients, especially when involved with canvassing!

Similarly, a negotiator involved in a much longer-term negotiation spread over, say, several months (e.g. the purchase of natural gas from the Norwegians), will need to adopt a softer, inductive role.

We should also bear in mind two other influences:

1. Making the relationship work

If your opponent is a natural extrovert who fills the time with lots of communication, you may find yourself in competition for 'air time'. If this were to continue unabated, it could lead to increasing frustration, talking over each other and, eventually, conflict.

If two negotiators whose natural styles lie in the extreme areas of the inductive style were to meet to discuss a case, there could be many questions asked by one party only to be met with more questions from the other!

In practice, people tend to use a mix of both styles, with plenty of give and take. In fact, the skilled negotiator will aim to develop expertise in both areas, so that he or she has complete flexibility and can move in and out of either approach depending on the needs of the opponent.

2. General cultural influences

Over the past decade, there has been a general move towards the inductive style in management and society in general. This may be attributable to a variety of influences:

- political neutralizing of some of the aggressive influences in the field of industrial relations
- increased awareness of the importance of meeting the needs of others

ι effects of the human relations school of management theory
● increased effects and support of management training.

TIP

Negotiators who are working in cultures other than their own need to adapt their style to suit the local customs and culture.

Who is my opponent?

We have seen that knowing something about your opponent before the meeting will be an advantage to any negotiator. If we have met the person before, we will be able to predict some of the possible levers and arguments which might be successful in the next round of discussions.

Aspects of communication style have already been discussed and we will now consider possible pressure points that could be applied to the debate.

All negotiations take place against a background of 'needs'; if needs did not exist, then there would be little point in meeting to negotiate. To help you prepare for the meeting, it would be useful to consider the needs of your opponent in more depth. There may also be a hidden agenda which will help you select a negotiation strategy.

The famous industrial psychologist Abraham Maslow (1908–70) identified a **hierarchy of needs** to explain why people are motivated to work in a modern industrialized environment:

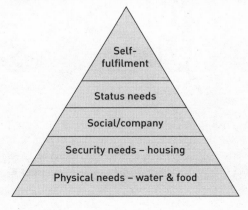

The broad concept of the triangle is that we all need to survive, by satisfying the needs at the base of the triangle. Having satisfied these **physiological** needs our attention turns to the need for **security**, satisfied through the provision of adequate housing/accommodation. Both these factors may be satisfied through the earning of money, but the higher motivators such as **social needs**, **status** and **self-fulfilment** are not usually satisfied in this way.

The model is shown as a triangle to illustrate the fact that not everybody reaches the higher needs – indeed, some people become hooked on one particular need.

For example, your opponent may have a particularly liking for good food and, therefore, may be a lot more malleable after a good meal (at your expense, of course!). Others may be especially 'hooked' on status symbols and quickly identify your deal as a way in which they can be successful and earn a bigger company car or a status jump in the firm's hierarchy.

Equally manipulative is the industrial-relations negotiator who holds a little in reserve to allow an opponent to feel victorious just when the union branch is about to re-elect its representatives or the management is considering the regrading of personnel professionals.

So where should we meet?

At first sight, this is a common-sense matter. Sales representatives might say that they always expect to go to visit the buyer, and the management side of a joint industrial council might always expect to hold meetings in the boardroom.

Actually, the place of the meeting can make quite a difference to its 'comfort factor'. Some people seem to be able to fit into any environment and still behave confidently in business meetings. Others are intimidated by the very thought of having to negotiate on the opponent's ground.

So, playing 'home' or 'away' may have advantages to you and your opponent:

'Home' advantages

- You can control interruptions.
- You can orchestrate recesses.
- Back-up support is available should you need it.
- You can choose the office/location/ layout to suit you.

'Away' advantages

- You may have the moral advantage in cases of late arrivals, etc.
- You have the chance to assess your opponent's workplace.
- Your opponent may make allowances as you are not on home ground.
- You can pressurize your opponent by suggesting that senior staff get involved to break any deadlocks.

Another alternative is to choose neutral territory. But, once again, there may be some hidden advantages. For example, the lobby of a hotel may appear to be neutral until you discover that your opponent is a regular visitor there and is personally known to the manager, the restaurant manager, the head porter, the barman and even the waitress. This can be most impressive – and is intended to be!

Will any of this make any difference to the meeting? It could do. After all, if you are dependent on your opponent for a crucial piece of information on which to base the negotiated agreement, would you mistrust someone who is so obviously credible in this sophisticated environment?

Summary

Developing our 'people skills' may need time and patience, but the payback will be really worth the effort and the progress steps suggested below may help you achieve better results:

- Try to develop a greater interest in other people – what they have to say, and their experiences.
- Build up your own self-confidence as you show you are a good listener.
- Learn how to reveal a little more of your own personality.
- Develop your questioning skills, especially those 'open' questions – the 'Whats', 'Wheres', Whens' and 'Hows', but not too many of the 'Whys' as they can seem confrontational.

You will find that, as people respond better to your conversations, they will talk more openly about their needs, making it much easier for you to show ways that these can be met.

Use the following sheet to help you plan your style and negotiation venue:

SUNDAY
MONDAY
TUESDAY
WEDNESDAY
THURSDAY
FRIDAY
SATURDAY

PLAN YOUR STYLE AND NEGOTIATION VENUE

What do you know about your opponents?

_____
_____
_____
_____

Who will be involved?

_____
_____
_____
_____

Their preferred style:

_____
_____
_____
_____

Your preferred style:

_____
_____
_____
_____

Possible venues

Home: _____   Away: _____

Neutral ground: _____

Who will need to be briefed?

1 _____

2 _____

3 _____

4 _____

Now try our multiple-choice questions to see how you have progressed.

For each question, choose *one preferred answer* (tick the box), then go to the answers at the end of the book to score your choices.

If you chose second (or even third) best answers, then think about why these answers are not as good as our 'top-rated' one.

Now turn to the end of the book and make a commitment to your Personal Action Plan.

SUNDAY
MONDAY
TUESDAY
WEDNESDAY
THURSDAY
FRIDAY
SATURDAY

Progress check (answers at the back)

1. Negotiation issues may be centred on the past or present but the results of the meeting will be most important to:
    a) Present issues and activities ❑
    b) Settlement of past difficulties ❑
    c) Future relationships ❑
    d) Past, present and future ❑

2. Talking persuasively by negotiators is best achieved by:
    a) Becoming a good listener ❑
    b) Improving your questioning skills ❑
    c) Concentrating on being positive ❑
    d) Exploiting an irresistible personality ❑

3. Having high aspirations in negotiation means:
    a) Trying to achieve win/win deals that are better than just 'average' ❑
    b) Being positive – even when there seems little to be positive about ❑
    c) Thinking clearly under stress ❑
    d) Being prepared to be 'pushy' ❑

4. An extrovert personality will be most effective in negotiating with an opponent who:
    a) Uses an inductive communication style ❑
    b) Enjoys stirring things up in a conversation ❑
    c) Uses an extrovert style ❑
    d) Is able to extend the ideas of others ❑

5. The application of a typical extrovert style in negotiating can result in:
    a) A 'tit-for-tat' competition in successive meetings ❑
    b) Opponents concentrating on all the negative aspects of a proposal ❑
    c) Outstanding results – especially if power is on that person's side ❑
    d) 'Bruised' feelings on the part of the opponent if feeling obliged ❑

6. Inductive-style negotiators benefit from:
    a) Revelations of focused information which may contradict the claims of the extrovert/uncontrolled negotiator ❑
    b) More thorough exploration of options ❑
    c) A general shift away from the extreme extrovert style in business culture ❑
    d) Shorter, but open, conversations with opponents ❑

7. The style of communication you choose to use in a negotiation should be determined by:
    a) The personality you have developed over the years ❑
    b) The outcomes you are trying to achieve ❑
    c) The communication style of your opponent ❑
    d) Your skills in asking/ answering questions ❑

8. Self-knowledge
a) Makes it more difficult to influence the other person because you over-identify with their 'problem' ❑
b) Enables you to get your own way in a negotiation ❑
c) Guarantees that you know when to 'back off' ❑
d) Enables you to recognize when you are in the presence of a rather better opponent ❑

9. An analysis of the underlying needs of your opponent may reveal:
a) Weaknesses in their case ❑
b) Needs which you could satisfy with the current offer ❑
c) 'Pressure points' which may persuade them into a deal ❑
d) Opportunities to build the relationship over a longer time ❑

10. The venue of the meeting should always be:
a) Agreed as part of the planning for the negotiation ❑
b) On 'home' territory ❑
c) Alternate – home or away – to be fair ❑
d) Somewhere both parties are comfortable ❑

WEDNESDAY

Breaking the ice

As with many other business functions, negotiation results are influenced considerably by your planning effort (and, conversely, disappointing results are often caused by inadequate preparation).

In the past three days' study we have explored the foundation plan of the meeting. Now it is time to open our meeting and begin the communication (talking, listening and non-verbal communication) which we hope will ultimately lead to an agreement.

Sometimes these foundations may seem to be ignored by experienced operators, who still achieve good results. However, for the less experienced, it would be a mistake to jeopardize or compromise good results by cutting corners when planning a negotiation.

It is a mistake to undervalue the part that good presentation can play in setting the scene for the meeting and in making proposals, and it is easy to see why good communicators might believe that the preparation stages are less important. However, it has been said that, if you fail to plan, you risk planning to fail! This can come as quite a shock to a persuasive communicator.

The way in which negotiators 'break the ice' at the start of a negotiation can have a big effect on the later stages of the meeting – so we are going to explore the twin aspects of:

- opening the meeting
- communicating.

Skills assessment

Results from the opening and the development of the early
stages of a meeting will be affected by the following factors.
Before working through today's pages, you might like to
rate your current skills in each of these areas by circling
the rating that you feel applies (and you might consider
obtaining a comparison with the ratings of someone who
knows you well):

Factor	Rarely used				Always used
Establishing rapport – verbal and non-verbal	1	2	3	4	5
Establishing common ground	1	2	3	4	5
Exploring mutual objectives for the meeting	1	2	3	4	5
Building a joint agenda	1	2	3	4	5
Getting comfortable	1	2	3	4	5
Clarity of speech	1	2	3	4	5
Assertive behaviour	1	2	3	4	5
Avoidance of bias and tunnel vision	1	2	3	4	5
Maintaining flexibility	1	2	3	4	5
Listening for overtones and signals	1	2	3	4	5
Questioning skills	1	2	3	4	5
Controlling and reading body language	1	2	3	4	5

Your performance in each of these areas can be improved and
will affect your results.

Opening the meeting

Creating the right atmosphere for the meeting will be
important if it is to end in agreement. Tough issues can
be sorted out without necessarily establishing an ice-cold

atmosphere at the start; equally, if the players have not met before and the stakes are high, quite some time may be allocated to establishing an atmosphere of trust.

Establishing rapport

The initial contact between people who are meeting for the first time – or, indeed, who have met before – is normally accompanied by an appropriate choice of words and actions.

However, the way these things are done can be significant. Passing the time of day and, as important, using your opponent's name, are accepted customs in greeting – just as shaking hands provides an acceptable way of expressing warmth to the other person. We make some hidden judgements on the basis of these greetings:

- the firmness of the handshake – the 'crusher' or the 'wet fish'
- the distance between the parties when they shake hands
- the formality or informality of the greeting – varying from 'Good morning' to 'Hi' or 'G'day'
- the warmth of the facial expression when meeting – for example, smiles can be open or, perhaps, cynical
- the extent of eye contact – open and level, or hooded and uncertain
- the appearance of the parties – the manner of dress and so on.

The golden rule in the area of appearance – for the best results – is to try not to breach any areas of known preference on the part of your opponent.

Common ground

It is always easier negotiating with someone you have met before because you will have some knowledge of that person's domestic circumstances, leisure interests, last holiday and/or drive or motivation. The early stages of a meeting provide an excellent opportunity to catch up with what has been happening in your respective lives – domestically and, probably more importantly (from the point of view of the negotiation), in business – since you last met.

This episode should help both parties to rebuild common ground, which may be especially valuable if (or when) the going gets tough later in the meeting.

Obviously, a new contact needs careful nurturing, and the opportunity should be taken to find out a little about them without creating the impression of being either nosey or pushy.

The agenda

It is surprising how often negotiators get together with a mutual interest in meeting but without having established a common agenda at the start. This is probably because each negotiator tends to think of their own agenda as of paramount importance and superior to the other person's.

If the meeting is to be collaborative, then it is important to provide the opportunity for both participants to air their own agenda. Apart from anything else, it is quite a challenge to check your opponent's agenda against the items you expected to be raised when you prepared for the meeting!

This does not mean that every agenda item or objective has to be revealed at the start of the meeting, but failure to do so in a collaborative atmosphere will invite scepticism: 'Why was this item concealed? Was it really a slip of the memory or has some advantage been sought by failing to reveal the topic?'

Physical comfort

The physical conditions of the meeting will also influence how comfortable (and possibly how co-operative) either party may feel, and this can be transferred readily to comfort with the deal itself. A variety of tactics may be adopted to win 'unfair' advantage over the opponent.

These usually work only when they are not too obvious, and, by virtue of their exposure, they tend to become less effective the more they are used. Examples are:

- your opponent's chair set at a lower level than yours
- your opponent having to look into the sun (or bright light)
- orchestrating interruptions when the going gets rough
- manipulating the temperature of the meeting room
- choosing a venue for the meeting which has distracting furnishings (e.g. walls decorated in, say, a vivid blue can affect some people and may account for an opponent disagreeing with proposals)
- prominent positioning of a clock, which may give discussions a sense of time pressure.

How should you deal with these tricks if and when they arise?

In short, the best method is to let your opponent see that you have noticed the tactic and seek his/her approval to remove the influence. You can do this by correcting or neutralizing the influence and commenting on it to allow your opponent to understand that you have noticed the use of the tactic.

Communicating

The most obvious skills are sometimes those which cause most difficulty in meetings. The effectiveness of the talking and listening process is affected by a variety of factors:

- self-discipline in allowing your opponent to speak (giving them some 'air-time')
- the style you use in speaking (e.g. not too biased or self-opinionated)
- quality of listening, which is affected by factors such as interpretation and concentration
- your body language.

Talking

From our earliest years, talking is essential to our well-being, but how we talk in a negotiation meeting can have quite an effect on how we are perceived by those we meet. For example, the following request to the boss would probably be greeted by a simple 'No!':

> 'I suppose it wouldn't be possible – I know this is probably not the best time to ask – to maybe find five minutes to get together to see if you could find your way clear to, perhaps, pay me an extra £10 per week?'

A great deal of work has been done recently on helping people develop assertiveness skills – the example above demonstrates non-assertive behaviour: vague, apologetic and almost defeatist. Few skilled negotiators would contemplate using this approach.

Equally, making the following demand:

> 'If you don't pay the yard staff an extra £10 per week, you will be looking for a new team!'

could result in the response:

> 'If that's your attitude, then perhaps that is the best thing for us to do!'

Skilled negotiators are more likely to use the following approach:

Negotiator 1: When will the Board be looking at this year's pay review?

Negotiator 2: It is scheduled for consideration in March.

Negotiator 1: How much are you proposing to include in the budget?

Negotiator 2: We will be under great pressure to find anything – given the present state of the market. How could the staff side make a contribution?

Negotiator 1: If you are talking about productivity improvement, the staff need money on the table! However, if you have something to offer, there may be scope for discussion.

Assertive expression is based on our needs, and the use of 'we' is better than 'I'. In fact, self-opinionated negotiators who use an egotistical approach often find it difficult to persuade others to change their minds or adopt their proposals.

Similarly, emotional responses are best kept under control. The use of anger, for example, can make a short-term point in a meeting, but if it is overused it can obstruct a negotiated settlement – with a 'lose/lose' result.

 The golden rule is to keep cool, avoid rhetoric and provocative language and maintain self-control.

This can be difficult if your opponent is hyped up and determined to cause maximum disruption as a deliberate tactic. In such cases, a good defence is to slow down interaction, make a conscious effort to avoid reaction and concentrate on non-confrontational language.

Listening

To say that it is essential to listen to interaction in negotiation meetings is to state the obvious. However, this can be harder than it seems. For a start, the process in any conversation can be difficult for some people; and when we are seeking a negotiated bargain it is complicated by the additional demands on our brain in the meeting.

Case study

Negotiator 1 makes a proposal to Negotiator 2, who listens carefully to the point. However, as the statement is unfolding, Negotiator 2 seeks to comprehend the point made – checking it against prior knowledge and experience and listening for the overtones in the expression – while also beginning to form a suitable reply and use an appropriate method (e.g. 'Shall I ask a question, make a statement or what?'). It is hardly surprising that points are missed in such circumstances – and sometimes our response may be totally irrelevant! (How well do you listen to your partner at home?)

How else can 'listening' go wrong? People have a habit of 'tuning out' – especially if they do not want to hear what is being said (try telling your teenage children to tidy their bedrooms, for example!). Others turn a deaf ear, making the right sounds while their brain is not really engaged and and without having a real commitment to change.

And, lastly, we take the power of vocabulary for granted – especially the importance of using comprehensible language. Jargon, for example, needs to be avoided and it is essential that any words that are not understood by the opponent are immediately clarified. Here, again, is another valuable use of assertive questioning.

Tips for improving your listening skills include the following:

- Watch your opponent's lips while they are talking (and watch their eyes while you are talking – to gauge their reaction to what you are saying).
- Try to concentrate on the overriding message in their contributions, rather than becoming bogged down or distracted by individual words.
- Take notes to aid your concentration.

- Avoid trying to second-guess your opponent's statements or trying to finish off their sentences (even in unison!).
- Categorize contributions received from your opponent (e.g. 'Is this contribution a question, summary or proposal?') and plan an appropriate response.

These approaches will improve your concentration and enable you to spot opportunities for discussion and for bargaining. For example, an innocuous discussion during the earlier part of a meeting with a client might reveal some interesting snipets of information:

1   'Yes, things have been pretty busy – we have just changed our computer system.'
2   'What kind of pressures has this brought? Strings of noughts on payslips?'
1   'No, but our bought ledger system came to a halt ...'

If you are proposing to supply this customer with a service or goods, be careful. You may decide on a contract easily enough, but may then have problems encouraging them to pay up! So, this signal should be followed up when it comes to agree terms of the contract at the end of the meeting.

Non-verbal communication

There are many other ways of communicating.

Body language, and the skill of reading it, has recently become a very popular topic among the business community. The reasoning goes something like this: 'If we could read the minds of our opponents and be able to work out exactly what they are thinking and planning, we could achieve much better deals!' Unfortunately, it is not as easy as that because analysing body language is an imprecise science.

That said, there are some simple signals that are useful to observe in negotiation, although the novice should be careful not to apply the meanings too literally in every situation.

Face touches
In a conversation about, say, the price of a service or goods, if the speaker accompanies a price quotation with a typical statement such as 'This is my best offer' with a rub of the nose, a scratch of the chin, a wipe of the eye or a tug at the collar, it may be an untruth! The chances of this being so increase if a chain of these actions occurs one after the other.

However, it should always be remembered that the speaker may have a cold (causing a constant nose irritation) or be feeling uncomfortable in a hot environment (hence the tug at the collar).

SUNDAY

MONDAY

TUESDAY

WEDNESDAY

THURSDAY

FRIDAY

SATURDAY

TIP *The moral here is that, while it is sensible to observe and try to read your opponent's body language, it is best not to allow your hands too near your face while negotiating!*

Eye gaze

Level eye contact is often taken as an indication of honesty and, therefore, an interpretation could be that the negotiator may be trusted. However, if a gaze is held in one direction too intently, it may be interpreted as staring! Negotiators need to vary their use of eye contact, but it is essential when looking for reactions to ideas or trial proposals. Failure to make eye contact may protract a meeting simply because the signals showing that your opponent is prepared to accept your position go unnoticed. What signals? The occasional frown or flicker of a smile; the raising of an eyebrow or even the sharp return of a glance. We take many of these actions for granted, but, if observed, they may help us interpret progress in the negotiation.

Mirroring

Two people who are anxious to make a good impression on each other with the aim of a win/win deal may mirror each other's body position and movements. The explanation for this is that each party is sending signals to convince their opponent that they are very similar in terms of attitudes, values and aims.

 TIP *This approach can have a significant effect, although it may only be subconscious. So, if your meeting is rather cold and you wish to try to relax your opponent, mirroring their body positioning may have a positive effect.*

Hand movements

Many people speak with their hands and, while this is quite natural, it is important that such movements do not become extravagant or distracting to your opponent. A pen or pencil can provide a useful means of underlining a point – especially if the meeting has become emotional – but aggressive movements should be eliminated. Anything which causes irritation in an opponent is to be avoided as it may lead to non-acceptance of your proposals.

In general, open-handed expressions may be taken to underpin the sincerity of the speaker, whereas pointing or closed fists may reveal aggressive undertones in your opponent.

Summary

Today's chapter has explored the foundations of communication between the two parties in some detail, and it would be surprising if your self-examination has not identified some improvement goals which you might incorporate into the Personal Action Plan at the back of the book.

We tend to take communication skills for granted and recognize that we could improve them only when we come across an opponent who is significantly better at it than we are (or when there is a major misunderstanding with our nearest and dearest!). Why not revisit the self-assessment at the beginning of Tuesday's chapter to check whether you need to update those grades, adding crosses against the target numbers (above your previous scores).

Now try our multiple-choice questions to see how you have progressed.

For each question, choose *one preferred answer* (tick the box), then go to the answers at the end of the book to score your choices.

If you chose second (or even third) best answers, then think about why these answers are not as good as our 'top-rated' one.

Now turn to the end of the book and make a commitment to your Personal Action Plan.

SUNDAY
MONDAY
TUESDAY
WEDNESDAY
THURSDAY
FRIDAY
SATURDAY

Progress check (answers at the back)

1. Opening a meeting or discussion will be much more effective if there is already an agreement about:
   a) Its purpose ❏
   b) The agenda ❏
   c) Who should attend ❏
   d) The venue for the meeting ❏

2. Confirming the purpose of the meeting at the start will help:
   a) Make everyone feel welcome ❏
   b) Ensure that everyone is at the right meeting ❏
   c) Enable additional items to be added to the agenda ❏
   d) Ensure that everyone knows the range of contribution they should be making ❏

3. Establishing rapport means:
   a) Concentrating on speaking the same 'language' as your fellow attendees ❏
   b) Getting on the same 'wavelength' as your colleagues at the meeting ❏
   c) Reading other people's body language ❏
   d) Being able to look one other in the eye ❏

4. How you open the meeting can have a big impact on the level of trust you are able to build up and, consequently:
   a) How open your colleagues might be to accepting new ideas or refining/improving established ones ❏
   b) How long the meeting will take to reach its objectives ❏
   c) The acceptability of any new ideas proposed at the meeting ❏
   d) The level of agreement everyone is prepared to give ❏

5. Building common ground with your opponent involves:
   a) Ensuring that you are wearing clothes that will not offend the other person ❏
   b) Avoiding any extreme language or subject matter that might offend your guests ❏
   c) Concentrating discussion on the main agenda subject ❏
   d) Sitting close together so that everyone feels committed to the meeting's objectives ❏

6. Listening to your opponents in a negotiation is easier if you:
   a) Like them ❏
   b) Are committed to the subject they are talking about ❏
   c) Achieve a balanced talk/listen ratio ❏
   d) Are able to ignore the distractions around you ❏

7. The agenda is the main guide for discussion topics at a negotiation meeting, and the main negotiators should:
a) Avoid all other topics ❏
b) Listen carefully for any new information which could have a bearing on outcomes/relationships between the parties ❏
c) Be prepared to add in their own (additional) topics, especially if it seems likely they will be agreed upon ❏
d) Avoid any discussion without a complete written agenda being agreed at the start ❏

8. It is best if the negotiator takes the lead by dominating the discussion and doing most of the talking
a) Wrong – both parties need to have their say ❏
b) It is better to aim for a fair/natural balance (e.g. 55 to 45 per cent) ❏
c) Correct, as being dominated could mean 'losing' ❏
d) It is best to leave the conversation to take its own course ❏

9. Analysing non-verbal communication (or body language) is overrated
a) Wrong – it can indicate issues which need clarifying or tackling ❏
b) Correct – people should feel that they can behave naturally and not worry about being misread ❏
c) Sometimes – uninhibited behaviour can be more persuasive ❏
d) It requires expert training and disciplined observation ❏

10. Negotiators who use hand movements to emphasize speech in negotiation meetings:
a) Can distract the listener and mislead them ❏
b) Should always be encouraged to behave naturally ❏
c) Provide additional information which may signal issues for greater exploration ❏
d) Should be encouraged to sit on their hands ❏

THURSDAY

The agenda

Having opened our negotiation and made some inner judgements about the other party, we need to make some progress in discussing our agenda. Of course, this should be in the other party's interest too, and if this does not seem to be the case then the need for the meeting should be reassessed.

Could it be that you have a reluctant partner to this negotiation – and, no matter how hard you try, the outcome will be a 'lose/lose'? The 'loss' may just be some time and effort – salespeople sometimes describe unwilling clients as 'time-wasters' – although their failure to 'qualify the customer' (ask questions to determine their interests, needs, preferences, timing, budget, etc.) in the first instance may have led directly to this situation.

Needs

We know that negotiation meetings are about resolving (or meeting) mutual needs. For example:

● you need to buy a new car and the dealer needs to sell one

or

● you need to obtain the reinstatement of a suspended work colleague and the management needs to obtain staff support for overtime to meet a rush order.

On Wednesday we found that discussion meetings provide the opportunity for us to present our side of the case – to promote and defend our interests, to sell our position and the advantages of accepting it to the other side.

We will also have tried to draw from our opponent a description of their position so that we can begin to debate it, undermine it and make it seem impossible or unreasonable. While this is going on, our opponent may be trying the same tactic on us!

Example

A standard tactic when surveying a second-hand car is to fault the car by referring to the high mileage, worn tyres or rust-marked body. This softening-up process is designed to precede the making of a proposal or offer (often a rather low one!), but this tactic may be easily rebuffed if the vendor is prepared to cite the 'large number' of other potential buyers who have been in touch about the car. Is the buyer really interested, or not?

Assertive questions such as 'How can you justify this position?' may draw your opponent to reveal his or her arguments and aims in the negotiation. With persistent questions, difficulties in arriving at a mutually agreed strategy on his or her side may be revealed, thus enabling you to take the high moral ground or express the stronger (more persuasive) argument.

Dividing your opponent from his or her side becomes easier once you know that there may have been some difficulty on their part in arriving at an agreed negotiating strategy.

Of course, such debating points are reversible and you must be careful not to lay yourself open to the use of this approach by your opponent. So, in our example outlined above, any

attempts by the vendor of the car to sell it to your partner – who is loudly proclaiming enthusiasm for the vehicle – may cause you some difficulty when it comes to obtaining the best price or terms.

In reality, it is unlikely that your opponent will make any major moves for nothing, so you will need to demonstrate your preparedness to move in some way as a means of obtaining movement from your opponent. These signals should have been sent and received before beginning to form the proposals or offers that will lead to the final bargain.

Proposing

Today's session describes how to maintain progress in the meeting by making appropriate proposals. We will consider:

- timing
- encouranging proposals
- the best formula
- defending principles
- meeting inhibitions.

All your preparation will prove its value in this vitally important stage.

Timing

There is a right time for proposals in a negotiation meeting, and experienced negotiators sense when the moment is right. This sense of timing is akin to the salesperson's ability to choose the right moment to close the sale. How we find this out, other than by trial and error, is analysed below.

Exhausting every avenue of discussion will eventually lead you to a stage when you have to make progress in the meeting, and making proposals is the next obvious step. However, this approach can feel overcautious and pedestrian, and may lead your opponent to become exasperated owing to the lack of

progress. (This can, of course, be turned to an advantage if
your opponent is very anxious to conclude the meeting – a
process which might be speeded up if he or she makes some
quick and major concessions.)

When your meeting concerns an urgent issue and either or
both negotiators have a strong sense of destiny, there will be an
irresistible force moving the discussion towards agreement –
especially if the parties have already expressed a strong desire
to reach an agreement. In such a situation, proposals will flow
naturally almost as a summary of each party's position.

The reverse of this natural progression rests in the truism
described by Professor Parkinson (referred to as Parkinson's
Law) – that time taken for decisions is in inverse proportion
to the costs incurred. Committees have been known to spend
hours taking decisions about the replacement of canteen cups
but only minutes on major decisions which few members

understand! The same can be true of negotiation: when small issues combine with ready quantities of time, progress in the meeting can be very slow – with as much attention given to the social objectives as the deal itself!

Finally, beware of the use of time as a major tactic in the meeting. Logical movement through the early stages of the meeting may be unattractive to so-called skilled negotiators, and this may lead to one of them suggesting a jump from base square to final square in one move. A simple, innocuous question might be asked:

- 'We are both busy people and I am sure we could close this deal very quickly – if you agree, of course?'
- 'Yes, that seems a good idea.'
- 'So, what is your bottom line?'

Revealing this position may make it difficult for the opponent to trade movement once the base position has been revealed. There will then be little alternative to agreeing to the initiator's proposals without breaking off negotiations altogether.

Encouraging proposals

If you feel that the time is right for proposals to be made but are not sure whether this feeling is mutual, you can always ask! Hand-holding skills (i.e. encouraging the opponent to feel that you are trustworthy and are not trying to lay a trap) are valuable in negotiation. Apart from giving the other side the opportunity to drive the meeting, encouraging them to make leading proposals in an open atmosphere will help progress to be made.

Such a step needs to be accompanied by appropriate non-verbal signals – warm smiles, gentle nods and a high level of attention (eye contact and slightly laid-back body position but facing the opponent).

Who should make the first proposal – and what that should be – is an issue which can give the inexperienced negotiator some concern. After all, there is little pleasure in feeling that your first 'bid' was too high and, having seen the speed with which the other party accepted, that you are paying more than you needed to!

A major aim of the early discussion stage in the meeting is to tease out the other party's position on each agenda item – and the arguments used to defend them. This may well indicate that, say, the vendor's preferred price is going to be totally beyond the resources of the buyer and some concessionary proposal is necessary to keep the buyer in the meeting. (A similar argument can be advanced for the buyer who tries to introduce a very low offer – risking insulting the vendor.)

So, the opening stance is recognized as the position that would bring most benefit for the proposer's party – the debate will doubtless seek movement towards the opponent's position – and the best format for this is when both parties move towards each other, trading concessions.

The best formula

Phrasing of proposals is crucial. The best formula is to present your proposals using a conditional approach. For example:

> '*If* you will give us payment terms of 30 days, *then* we will meet your price request.'

Now, this proposal may seem rather bald – especially without the context of the earlier conversation. When a bridge is needed between the discussion part of the meeting and concluding the bargain, either party may introduce **trial proposals**. These will suggest tentative ways forward without necessarily burning boats and risking earlier agreement by suggesting something which is not acceptable to the opponent.

A typical example would be:

> 'I'll tell you what we might be able to arrange: *if perhaps* you could find a way of speeding up payment – say, in 30 days – *then we might* be able to find a way of reducing the price.'

If this approach brings a constructive response, then it is likely to be followed swiftly by a formalized proposal along the lines of the first example above.

Defending principles and meeting inhibitions

It is at this stage that you may find your bottom line under attack or under threat of being compromised. For example, the UK Government made it clear after the Falklands War in 1982 that sovereignty was not even on the agenda for peace negotiations with Argentina, and that this would be a precondition for any future discussions.

There could be a risk that, while such a condition might be agreed, your opponent may reintroduce that element in the meeting itself, with the expectation that the constructive atmosphere might persuade negotiators to allow discussion of the issue. This clearly should not be accepted and the team would have to make it clear that approaches to put the subject on the agenda would jeopardize agreements on other issues.

At the same time, you must remember that your opponent is not an entirely free agent. He or she is representing another organization or party, with interests which may differ from your own. These interests will overlap – or there will be no point in attending the meeting – but it is obviously in your opponent's interests to persuade you to move from your ideal position.

Example

A client complains about one of your service engineers whose behaviour on his premises has been the source of complaint from several of his staff. His initial approach may be to demand the withdrawal of that person ('Never send him here again!'), and this may be readily countered with an apology and a convincing promise to hold a full and thorough internal inquiry.

However, if we were to think through our opponent's position we would see that his organization has in it several people who would also like to see the back of the engineer. Failure on his part to sort out the issue could lead to a significant loss of face and credibility for your opponent. Such inhibitions can lead to apparent obstinacy and may make a win/win agreement more difficult to achieve if the client's inhibitions are not addressed.

Summary

We have seen in today's chapter that proposals are vital to a negotiation, no matter how fundamental or extreme the issues under debate happen to be. There are many examples on record of negotiation teams becoming 'comfortable' in debating the issues, and conversation then seems to go round and round without any agreement or solution – except, maybe, an agreement for the location and timing of the next meeting!

If you find yourself to be a willing party to such a travesty, remember that senior management/leadership can always exercise its right to change the delegated negotiators. How might it feel and look to be one of the people who have been replaced so peremptorily?

So, proposals are what make the negotiation move forward, and they need to be carefully planned and thought through; not arrived at in desperation without any concern for how they might be implemented.

Once again, we invite you to try our multiple-choice questions to see how you have progressed.

For each question, choose one preferred answer (tick the box), then go to the answers at the end of the book to score your choices.

If you chose second (or even third) best answers, then think about why these answers are not as good as our 'top-rated' one.

Now turn to the end of the book and make a commitment to your Personal Action Plan.

SUNDAY
MONDAY
TUESDAY
WEDNESDAY
THURSDAY
FRIDAY
SATURDAY

Progress check (answers at the back)

1. The only way a negotiation can progress is through the use of:
   a) Signals ❏
   b) Collaborative relationships ❏
   c) Proposals ❏
   d) Summaries ❏

2. When is the 'right' time to start making proposals?
   a) Any time, discovered through a process of trial and error. ❏
   b) When the issue, which needs resolution, is urgent ❏
   c) When your 'opponent' starts proposing ❏
   d) When you have a good idea of the needs of the other party ❏

3. The statement 'Supposing we were able to offer a discount of 5 per cent, if you committed to this purchase today' is a:
   a) Dream ❏
   b) Signal that your opponent is ready to make a move ❏
   c) Proposal ❏
   d) Trial proposal ❏

4. Conditional proposals are based on the principle of:
   a) Something for something ❏
   b) Collaborative bargaining ❏
   c) Win/lose ❏
   d) 'If..., then...' ❏

5. If your proposal is rejected by the other party, this means:
   a) They want you to improve your offer in some way ❏
   b) The negotiation has failed. ❏
   c) You may have misunderstood their position and you need to clarify it ❏
   d) The other party has a better proposal of their own ❏

6. A very low offer or proposal could result in:
   a) Insulting your opponents, and their withdrawal ❏
   b) Beating your own objectives, if it is accepted ❏
   c) A breakdown in relationships between the parties ❏
   d) A great reputation as a principled negotiator ❏

7. Revealing that the value of a proposal lies outside your authority to accept shows that:
   a) Your opponent is talking to the wrong person ❏
   b) You have no better arguments ❏
   c) You have prepared a negotiation plan ❏
   d) A real obstacle exists to any agreement at this level ❏

8. People who prefer to make the first proposal invariably:
   a) Lose through revealing their hand too soon ❏
   b) Should be given a quick counter-proposal ❏
   c) Are surprised when it isn't accepted ❏
   d) Win through leading the argument ❏

9. Debating what seem to be minor points (and in considerable depth):

a) Risks frustrating both parties and the withdrawal of one party (i.e. lose/lose) ❏

b) May reveal a lack of confidence (or knowledge) ❏

c) May hide a hope to win by causing the opponent to give in ❏

d) May lead to the opponent complaining to your boss ❏

10. How should you react if your discussion reveals that your original preparation was inadequate?

a) Call a natural recess/break to enable you to catch up ❏

b) Seek help from your boss ❏

c) Quickly change the subject ❏

d) Withdraw from discussion to avoid making an expensive or embarrassing mistake ❏

FRIDAY

Concluding

As we review our progress through the five days we have spent:

- learning about key aspects of negotiating,
- how to move towards agreement and
- concluding it successfully

it may seem over-complicated when a street market negotiation may be concluded in a matter of minutes! Of the topic can have a big effect on the speed of progress in negotiating, but the skills we employ in street trading are closer to 'haggling' than to the professional style of debating the issues, seeking mutual movement and benefits, and ensuring that the agreement is worthwhile and long-lasting.

Few experienced negotiators can claim to have a totally trouble-free record in the deals they have arrived at (and then had to live with!).

Experience can be an expensive teacher and this fact is what makes this last stage in the negotiation so important – the need to be able to close the meeting with agreements that are satisfactory to both sides (and with both parties clear and committed to the next stage – implementation).

Closing skills

There is little point in investing time in negotiation meetings if we cannot close them with satisfactory agreements. However, there are many people in the commercial world who make presentations with a view to selling a product or service, or buyers who invest time in meeting with sales representatives without those meetings resulting in a contract.

The question is: do those involved ever discover why their closing rate is not higher? And can they do anything about it? In staff-relations meetings there is less priority given to immediate results – they are often broken by recesses and adjournments, consultations between staff representatives and their members, and between personnel staff and their managers. But the same discipline applies here – if time is invested in meetings, then agreement must be the ultimate objective.

So, what are the skills we need to develop to close off a negotiation meeting satisfactorily? The following checklist may provide useful insights:

- Summarizing progress ☐
- Resurrecting earlier issues for agreement ☐
- Linking issues in the agreement ☐
- Using concessions to improve the agreement ☐
- Listening for concessions ☐
- Using appropriate closing techniques. ☐

Mistakes at the 'last fence' can be very expensive and frustrating. Make sure that you are able to clear the last few hurdles cleanly so that you are satisfied with your performance!

Summarizing
One little word!

It is not possible to do too much summarizing in a meeting. The fact is that many people become confused during negotiations and, even though one party has a clear belief in what has been agreed, it often happens that the opponent has a very different view of that same agreement! Both people were at the same meeting and yet there is still confusion and little unanimity – and this is very dangerous when the agreement is actually implemented.

Examples of things going wrong after the negotiations have stopped are legion. Buyers select colours of merchandise and plainly state the colours they do not want – and yet, somehow, those colours still arrive in deliveries! Similarly, sales representatives inform buyers about discount terms, and yet buyers still claim, once the invoice arrives, that they were not told about them.

Summaries help to clarify proposals and the terms of agreement. You cannot have too many of them! Remember the one little word which provides the signal of a summary – **'so'** – and try to use it:

- whenever the meeting stops making progress
- when you are not sure what has been said or agreed
- when you feel that the time is right to begin to close the meeting.

Accuracy in summaries

When summaries are used in a meeting they can have an extraordinary effect. First, a summary often seems to fix the points stated and agreed – even though both sides know that

SUNDAY

MONDAY

TUESDAY

WEDNESDAY

THURSDAY

FRIDAY

SATURDAY

the discussion is not yet finished. This can be very helpful when seeking to make speedy progress, but it is important for the summary to be accurate. If you include in your summary something that has not been agreed – even if you feel that you are taking artistic licence – there is a risk that the relationship between the two parties will be broken and trust breached.

Similarly, it is very important to listen to summaries given by your opponent. There is always a risk that something you believe has been agreed is left out or changed in the opponent's summary. If this happens, it is important that the person who spots the error speaks out straight away, otherwise the change may be accepted into the agreement by default, and could cause major disruption towards the end of the meeting. This might not affect the ultimate agreement but it may leave either or both parties with a bad feeling and have a knock-on effect on future meetings.

TO RECAP, THEN – YOU'LL INCLUDE POSTAGE, GIFT WRAPPING AND A HOLIDAY IN MAURITIUS FOR MY WIFE & ME

Resurrection

By virtue of the fact that a strategic summary will be seen as a means of bringing the meeting towards a close, it provides a last opportunity to raise any items on which no progress was made earlier.

On Tuesday, you will have rated yourself on persistence. This is an important quality for negotiators. The fact is that people who refuse to move earlier in a meeting may be a little more flexible when the end of the meeting is in sight. Also, the presentation of your case and the subtle temptation of concessions may encourage your opponent to be more flexible on issues which were sticking points before.

Linking

Linking one item with another is another method of obtaining movement on difficult issues. Most negotiators see their agenda as consisting of a variety of separate issues or objectives – indeed, many commercial deals involve the sale and purchase of several products or items, each of which needs to have been negotiated. It would be quite normal for the negotiators to achieve different deals on each item on the list, but it is also likely that either side may resist giving way on one particular item. A way out of this is to link one issue with another.

SUNDAY
MONDAY
TUESDAY
WEDNESDAY
THURSDAY
FRIDAY
SATURDAY

Example

A buyer may have agreed to pay a wholesaler $11.00 for a box of five reams of photocopying paper with an order of 100 boxes. He is pleased with this agreement as the price agreed is 50 cents a box less than he had expected to have to pay. Another item on his shopping list is some specialized bond paper for use in preparing and presenting reports. The wholesaler has offered a price of $18.00 a box, to which the buyer is not prepared to agree – his counter offer is $16.00. On the basis of negotiating the same quantity of paper, the buyer offers to increase the price on the copy paper by 25 cents per box if the vendor will agree to a price of $16.00 for the bond.

YES, YOU **SAID** BLUE – BUT I COULD TELL YOU **REALLY** WANTED PINK

PINK

TIP

Remember that everything is negotiable and you just need to persuade the other side to accept this to make progress with issues on which your opponent has inhibitions.

Using concessions

Concessions may provide a way of obtaining additional movement towards the end of the meeting. Skilled negotiators know to keep additional concessions up their sleeves to use in closing the meeting. These will be most effective where the concessions are cheap for you to give but very valuable to your opponent.

> ## Example
>
> If you have just sold your car – and therefore have cleared the cheque – you may be able to persuade your garage to extend the warranty on a new car for the all-in price which you agreed earlier, but now with the additional concession of a cash transaction.

Closing

Salespeople are frequently trained in how to close the sale, and a variety of methods exist to help achieve just that. However, if negotiators have done their job well, the meeting will close itself. The best resolution of the meeting is when both parties have achieved what they set out to achieve (i.e. within the parameters of their objectives) and all that is left to do is to formalize the agreement.

This may not always happen, so it is sometimes necessary for the meeting to be nudged towards closure. Some common ways of achieving this are:

- calling a recess
- imposing a deadline
- threatening to pull out or call time
- asking for agreement
- the summary close.

Calling a recess

Making a decision about, and therefore committing to, the agreement that has been discussed often requires a little time and space. Reluctance from your opponent to agree to the deal

may be overcome by planting the seeds of satisfaction in his or her mind and then allowing time for thought (with a view to allowing the seed to mature and flourish). If you have covered the ground well and summarized the areas of agreement, a short recess at this stage should bring a positive decision.

Imposing a deadline

If there is any doubt about the result of the recess it might be prudent to lay down some rules about the time for which the current offer will be valid. Clearly, this approach may be viewed as pressurizing your opponent, but is quite justifiable when the time period is fair.

A typical example could be a quotation for a construction task that is dependent on the supply of the materials, for which the quotation assumes no price rises for the materials. Therefore the quoted price can be valid only for, say, one month.

Threatening to pull out

If one party believes that the other party needs the agreement, then a bluff to pull out of the meeting may work.

However, such orchestrated tactics can easily rebound on the bluffer if the timing or style of the threat is poor. You might easily find that you are allowed to go and are not called back!

On the other hand, it has been known for creative answers to be found to situations when the time has run out on the negotiating.

For example, when international negotiators spent 18 months trying to negotiate a Strategic Arms Limitation Treaty, and the self-imposed deadline was reached, the parties agreed to stop the clock for 36 hours – just sufficient time for the final agreement to be transacted. When they finished, the agreement was backdated to fit the original deadline!

Asking for agreement

A simple way of closing the deal is to ask for your opponent's agreement! At first sight, this is such an obvious approach that it may be unclear why everyone doesn't use it all the time. 'Asking for the order' is a classic technique taught on most sales training courses. However, salespeople do not often use the approach, simply because of the risks of being turned down.

Actually, a rejection might not be the disaster it may seem. It may be possible to rescue the deal even at a late stage simply by asking 'Why?'. The answer may clarify your opponent's objections, giving you one last chance to bring the negotiation to a satisfactory conclusion.

The summary close

Finally, the closing point for the meeting should be summarized. The skills for this have been described earlier today.

> **A cautionary note!**
>
> Don't forget that your opponent enjoys the freedom to agree or not to agree! Even though you may have worked hard and concluded a good deal, your opponent is still acting for his or her reasons, not yours. This may be worth bearing in mind if you are feeling euphoric when you start to evaluate the deal.

Confirming

Even when your meeting seems to have closed with a full-hearted agreement, there are still risks that the implementation of the agreement will be faulty. The success of the negotiation lies in this process and it is probably hard – with the euphoria of a successful outcome – to turn your mind to what can go wrong.

However, things do go wrong, often for no sinister reason. The parties' recollection of what was agreed may be inadequate, but if the performance of the agreement does not meet either sides' expectations it would be quite understandable if underlying motives were questioned.

Solutions to avoiding these problems include:

- taking and exchanging notes
- getting the agreement in writing
- checking that minutes and opponent's notes agree with your notes
- taking care with the small print.

Taking and exchanging notes

It isn't easy to contribute to a negotiation meeting – talking, listening and making notes – but working notes of the meeting will be an essential foundation for any subsequent agreement or contract. In the commercial world, it is quite usual for a representative's memorandum of sale and a buyer's order

SUNDAY
MONDAY
TUESDAY
WEDNESDAY
THURSDAY
FRIDAY
SATURDAY

to be drafted during the meeting and exchanged at the end. This provides the first check that both sides have a common understanding of what has been agreed and, with experience and trust built up over time, one side may be prepared to accept the other's notes.

In staff-relations meetings it is common for both parties to nominate their own secretary to take minutes of the meeting, and the notes are then used to form the ultimate record of the meeting.

Get it in writing!

Even when notes have been exchanged at the end of the meeting, it is still important for a formal record of the agreement to be exchanged. Most negotiations commit two organizations as well as the various players, and formal records will need to be exchanged.

Confirmations may take the form of:

- purchase requisitions
- sales order notes
- minutes of meetings
- letters of confirmation
- revised proposals (bringing letters of acceptance)
- formal contracts
- joint communiqués or treaties
- procedural agreements and bargains.

A cautionary check is to ask yourself: 'Am I covered in law if anything should go wrong? Who could I sue?' This is not to say that you would wish to sue – most disputes between contractors are resolved by negotiation. But skilled negotiators will not put themselves into a position where they have no recourse if the opponent should renege on the agreement.

Check confirmations agree with your notes

How often have you attended meetings and failed to recognize the minutes when they have been released some time later? Unfortunately, those who have the responsibility to prepare the notes are sometimes tempted to misuse that power to rewrite them to suit their preferred position – subsequent to the meeting. Even if deception is not intended, subtle changes may take place to meet the political inhibitions of the boss, the organization or even some of the people present. Where changes have been noted, and where these affect the letter or spirit of the agreement, a loud complaint should be made, officially. Any apathy here may be taken as acceptance of the new situation.

Take care with the small print

One major company in the north of England employs a whole department of lawyers whose main task is to check buying agreements and ensure that their own terms and conditions are supreme over those of their suppliers. The consequence of this is that any small supplier is unlikely to be able to achieve any variation to those terms and may be faced with the stark choice of contracting on the buyer's terms or not at all.

We would all prefer that contractual breakdowns did not lead to recourse to the law – this can be very expensive in time and money – but the larger the contract the better it would be to ensure that the worst consequences of failure do not leave you totally exposed to losses. For this reason, penalty clauses are often found in construction contracts, restraint of trade in personal contracts and even clauses allowing actions for damages against trade union bodies where the continuity of supply of a service is affected by a trade dispute.

Summary

A 'win/win' result is usually the objective of every negotiator who is aiming for repeat business and the building of goodwill. It matters not whether the sums or issues are small or gargantuan – alliances are built by mutual trust and benefit for both parties, and can be reflected on with mutual pride and trust.

This may sound trite, but it is not difficult to find cases where one party's greed or 'sharp practice' has led to the breakdown of trust, loss of repeat business or even court action (to say nothing of all that appalling publicity). No one in their right mind would want that, but the consequences of getting it wrong are what makes this negotiation skill so important (and the negotiator highly responsible).

It has been said that the combination of an industry-leading strategy and excellent negotiators can bring world-beating results. Unfortunately, the opposite is also true!

For the last time, try our multiple-choice questions to see how you have progressed.

For each question, choose *one preferred answer* (tick the box), then go to the answers at the end of the book to score your choices.

If you chose second (or even third) best answers, then think about why these answers are not as good as our 'top-rated' one.

Now turn to the end of the book and make a commitment to your Personal Action Plan.

SUNDAY

MONDAY

TUESDAY

WEDNESDAY

THURSDAY

FRIDAY

SATURDAY

Progress check (answers at the back)

1. When you hear the word 'so' you should:
   a) Ignore it – only your summary is important ❏
   b) Insist that what is said is put into writing before you agree ❏
   c) Listen carefully, as your opponent is about to summarize and you will need to reject it if you disagree with it ❏
   d) Be prepared to reject the proposal ❏

2. Resurrecting earlier issues towards the end of the meeting:
   a) Risks spoiling the whole agreement ❏
   b) May lead to a fuller agreement if the atmosphere is more constructive ❏
   c) Should be avoided for fear of causing the other party to walk out ❏
   d) Provides a way out of an impasse or stalemate ❏

3. When facing potential deadlock, a recess will:
   a) Be a waste of time ❏
   b) Enable both sides to relax ❏
   c) Create a solution for the final agreement ❏
   d) Provide an opportunity to do some creative thinking and maybe seek further information or advice ❏

4. In recognizing a degree of uncertainty/nervousness in your opponent's reluctance to reach agreement, the best option is to:
   a) Impose a time deadline ❏
   b) Threaten to put the matter to their senior management ❏
   c) Give specific reassurances on how any 'losses' will be mitigated (e.g. through guarantees) ❏
   d) Threaten to escalate the case to your senior management ❏

5. Forcing further concessions from the opposition after agreement has been reached (and on an issue that has been overlooked in discussion) would most likely:
   a) Enhance the final deal for one party at the expense of the other ❏
   b) Risk the whole agreement being cancelled ❏
   c) Cause the other party to 'lose face' ❏
   d) Achieve a great winning result ❏

6. A good measure of success in a negotiation is the number of concessions that could have been made but which remained unused.
   a) True ❏
   b) True if both parties become aware of the total picture ❏
   c) Totally untrue – it's the quality of the outcome that's important ❏
   d) Untrue – it's the level of goodwill that has been further enhanced by the agreement ❏

7. A satisfactory deal can sometimes be further improved by:
   a) Meeting on neutral territory ❑
   b) Exploring concessions that might not have been used by either side and that could be exchanged with mutual benefit ❑
   c) Negotiating over a meal (the other side paying the bill) ❑
   d) Having two different negotiators ❑

8. However good – and complete – the negotiation, the proof of its success lies in:
   a) The tactics used in the meeting ❑
   b) The way the deal sounds to the 'boss' ❑
   c) Both parties' understanding of the agreement ❑
   d) The written record ❑

9. Successful implementation of a negotiated agreement is nearly always dependent on:
   a) Both parties' commitment to the deal ❑
   b) The size of the deal ❑
   c) The degree of trust that has been built up between the negotiators ❑
   d) The scale of the risk of failure of implementation ❑

10. The 'best pairing' of negotiators occurs when:
    a) Both are committed to a win/lose outcome ❑
    b) Both are highly rated as effective negotiators and they recognize this in each other ❑
    c) Their styles of interaction are very similar ❑
    d) Their styles of interaction are fully compatible ❑

SATURDAY

Learning from your experiences

If life provides experiences from which we can learn and develop, this must be more true of negotiating than most other activities! However, human nature (being what it is) does not bring a guarantee that all of us learn from our experiences and apply those lessons. We have all met people who keep on repeating the same mistakes, even when those errors are blatantly obvious and pointed out to them. Is there anything we can do about this if it is in our nature?

Yes! When it comes to negotiating, there are things we can (and should) do – starting with self-reflection, better preparation and more self-discipline in developing the skills outlined in this book.

SUNDAY

MONDAY

TUESDAY

WEDNESDAY

THURSDAY

FRIDAY

SATURDAY

Evaluating performance

Consider the following checklist, which may help you pinpoint your own strengths and weaknesses.

Preparation

1 Do I spend enough time preparing to negotiate?
2 Have I discussed the case with other people in my organization?
3 Have I researched my opponent's case?
4 Is there any additional information I may be able to collect from my opponent's organization?
5 Which outcome do I really want: win/win, win/lose or lose/lose?
6 Have I prepared a negotiation plan/brief?
7 What is on my objectives/shopping list?
8 What are the parameters for each objective?
9 Have I prioritized my objectives?
10 What concessions can I give?
11 Where will we meet?
12 Have I analysed the relative power positions of our two organizations?
13 When will be the best time to meet?

Know yourself

14 In what circumstances am I:

- most comfortable?
- least comfortable?

15 How easy do I find it to:

- take decisions?
- persuade others?
- be positive and persistent?
- choose the most persuasive words?
- think clearly under stress?
- control myself?

16 What motivates me? What 'Achilles' heels' (weak points)
   might exist in me?
17 Am I a disciplined listener?
18 Am I tempted by a win/lose opportunity if I will be the winner?

Opening the meeting

19 How good am I at putting others at ease?
20 How good are my presentation skills?
21 Can I control and read body language?
22 How able am I to probe others for information?
23 Can I respond to others' probing without giving away
   anything of value?
24 How well am I able to develop a collaborative atmosphere
   in a meeting?
25 Have we established a common agenda and identified
   common ground?

The meeting

26 How well can I balance talking and listening?
27 How can I make the meeting layout work for me?
28 How good are my concentration and listening skills?
29 When might a recess be useful?
30 How can I make good use of interruptions?
31 Who is in control in the meeting?
32 Have I identified the best time to make proposals?
33 How good am I at introducing trial proposals?
34 How can I formulate counter-proposals to overtake my
   opponent's proposals?
35 Am I using 'If... then' and 'So...' successfully?
36 When my opponent blocks my proposals, am I able to
   unblock them again?
37 How able am I to use the following closing skills?

   ● hand-holding
   ● summarizing
   ● using late concessions
   ● linking

SUNDAY MONDAY TUESDAY WEDNESDAY THURSDAY FRIDAY SATURDAY

TIP *Don't forget that the real test of your negotiation meeting lies in the results, and that skilled negotiators have:*

- *a track record of significant success*
- *a low incidence of failure in the implementation of their agreements*
- *high ratings for effectiveness by both sides.*

Continuing to grow

Negotiation is a practical skill. It is subject to the same characteristics as other skills – it gets rusty if it is not used and improves when used frequently. So, there are a number of steps which you as a negotiator can take to increase these skills:

- Take every opportunity to negotiate.
- Talk about negotiation with experienced people both inside and outside your organization.
- Read about negotiation. Look at:

  - newspaper articles for recent cases
  - trade magazines for technical sources
  - books and articles.

- Review your deals carefully and thoroughly.
- Attend a training course that enables you to obtain some feedback about your style and skills (preferably through the use of video). We look forward to meeting you soon at one of our workshops!

The truth is rarely pleasant, but the review process will be pointless if you indulge in self-deception. Check your objectives and those of your opponent which you know about – and make sure that you do not make the same mistakes twice!

Finally, we wish you happy and successful negotiating!

SUNDAY

MONDAY

TUESDAY

WEDNESDAY

THURSDAY

FRIDAY

SATURDAY

7 × 7

Seven tips for new negotiators

1 Negotiation is now part of everyday life – judging the opportunities and applying the best methods is all important or the results may be disappointing at best and a waste of effort at worst.

2 Initially, work within your comfort zones (which means place, time, people and topics), especially when building your confidence. Outcomes will be affected by past experiences – and the more positive these are, the more likely you will be able to repeat them and 'grow'.

3 Identify your own weak areas of knowledge or facts – and give extra time and effort to these so that you have more positive information and persuasive arguments on hand to increase the chances of acceptance.

4 Timing is crucial – the most productive atmosphere is when both parties are anxious to achieve change. This should be built upon and exploited. (Rolling a heavy 'scheme' downhill is easiest; pushing liquid uphill is well-nigh impossible. So, be prepared to drop everything else when an opportunity for change presents itself.)

5 Make it easy on yourself by identifying and reducing any barriers. If you are invited to 'play away' (on your opponent's ground), build your strategy around winning tactics for that meeting. Don't give your opponent any excuses for rejecting your proposals or schemes by appearing to be 'stand-offish'.

6 Listen carefully to what is said (and what is *not* said), to your opponent's needs and to their response to your proposals. Seek clarification rather than mount an attack, and be persuasive with incontrovertible evidence to support your full scheme.

7 Be sensitive – use top 'people skills' in persuasion and avoid giving any impression of pressure, desperation... or weakness.

Seven best personal resources

1 Gavin Kennedy, *Negotiate Anywhere: Doing Business Abroad* (Hutchinson, 1986)
2 Dale Carnegie, *How to Win Friends and Influence People* (Vermillion, 2006) – a 'classic' and essential reading for all who seek to negotiate win/win deals.
3 Terry Gillen, *Positive Influencing Skills* (Institute of Personnel & Development, 1995) – offers alternative approaches to command and control – especially 'pulling' rather than 'pushing'
4 Thomas A. Harris, *I'm OK, You're OK* (Arrow, 2012) – a record-breaking US bestseller. Climb out of the cellar of your mind!
5 John E. Tropman, *Making Meetings Work: Achieving High-quality Group Decisions*, 2nd edition (SAGE, 2003)
6 Geoff Ribbens and Greg Whitear, *Body Language: How to Read People, Understand Office Politics and Uncover Deception* (Hodder Arnold)
7 Peter Fleming, *Advanced Negotiation Skills In A Week* (John Murray Learning, 2016) – the 'follow-up' text to this one, giving a more advanced overview of the skills involved and demonstrating how new skills can be applied in the pursuit of outstanding results

Seven things to do today

1 Revisit some recent deals and consider what created the differences between those that you would consider were win/win, win/lose or lose/lose.

2 How might the results have been made different? And how will you work differently as a result of this assessment?

3 Work out the relative bargaining power you have with another party – taking care that, if you use power to get your own way, sooner or later they will do the same to you. How else will you negotiate?

4 Develop your own method of backing your proposals with sound justification and arguments (e.g. using discreet notes in 'code' or 'shorthand'?).

5 Practise your listening – rather than talking; your questioning skills should be as strong as your 'selling' skills. (Yes, non-sellers need to be able to sell ideas, too!)

6 Try to develop your summarizing skills – regular summaries show that you have heard and understood what has been said. Skilled negotiators tend to emphasize the points that are helpful to their 'cause' while playing down other party's points which would not be so acceptable.

And an important 'don't'!

7 Don't show triumph! Especially when you think you have the better end of a deal. It could lead to your 'opponent' to become determined to gain revenge next time round.

Seven behaviours to avoid

1 Before you start: 'Don't talk yourself out of a deal!', so advises Carol Frohlinger of www.negotiatingwomen.com. This is good advice! It is your opponent's job to convince you that your scale of objectives is unrealistic.

2 When trying to be flexible – take care! Bill Coleman advises us: 'The worst thing you can say is "I want £x for this job," leaving no opening for negotiation by the other side. Better language is "I hope to earn between £X and £Y". That gives the other party more flexibility.' BUT: it may also be taken to have revealed your 'limits'. Wouldn't any buyer immediately 'attack' the bottom figure? And wouldn't any self-respecting salesperson 'attack' the top one?

3 Dangerous words: 'The single most dangerous word which can be spoken in business is 'no'! The second most dangerous word is 'yes'! says Lois Wyse. It is possible to negotiate without saying either! However, 'shadow-boxing' can be very frustrating. Don't overuse this strategy or the meeting may end in turmoil.

4 Lies: a presumption that lies will underpin negotiation encourages the thought that it will all be based on the win/lose culture. This could be very unhelpful in the case of building a long-term trading relationship.

5 Kidology: when things are going well, it is easy to assume that we might just be able to 'walk on water' and fix any negotiation! Success will come from a variety of factors – for example, the reputation of your product/service/company. Try to maintain a sense of balance – enjoy your success, but don't overlook the fact that your 'opponents' always have a choice.

6 To musician Marvin Gaye is attributed the saying: 'Negotiation means getting the best of your opponent.' Does it? This is a 'win/lose' strategy and very likely to rebound next time around.

7 'The most important trip you may take in life is meeting people halfway' is a commonly heard phrase. Halfway sounds fair enough but this depends on either party's limits – have these been disclosed?

Seven preliminary issues – your coach's suggestions

1 'In my "world" negotiation just doesn't happen... If I tried, I fear I would be made to look stupid, naive or even in the wrong business.'

Coach: 'Don't be negative... even if this were true, for most people any "wins" are likely to be a closely guarded secret. Otherwise, everyone would be encouraged to negotiate and make life harder for their opponents! So, build your case (be prepared with a fallback position in case of an outright rejection) and be as persuasive as you can – to achieve just a small concession. Once the "door" is opened, even better results could follow!'

2 'I wouldn't want people to think that I cannot afford the product or service...'

Coach: 'Don't worry about what people might think. Negotiating is more common than you might think and terms are often set with some room for manoeuvre by vendors or purchasers. If you don't try, you'll never know if you could have achieved a better deal!'

3 'How do you know when your "opponent" is prepared to negotiate?'

Coach: 'They'll probably send a "signal". For example, when discussing a price they may say "price depends on the quantity that you order". In other words: "We may discount the price if the quantity is sufficient." Ignoring such a signal can prove costly.'

4 'My contacts try to negotiate over everything. Am I doing something wrong or should I be working a different way?'

Coach: 'Their senior management may have imposed tough expectations as the economy has toughened. Once this is explained and proved, both buyers and sellers can usually find ways of helping each other with new ideas/proposals. If there are no good reasons established for seeking flexibility in prices/quantities, any negotiator has the right to refuse.'

5 'Isn't success in negotiating dependent on the relative power between the parties – and the small/weak party is likely to "lose" by making all the concessions?'

Coach: 'Not necessarily – "small" can mean exclusive and highly desirable as a partner; many businesses started out with this strategy and quickly gained support from other organizations with similar marketing strategies. This approach can lead to impressive growth in the marketplace!'

6 'Time is money in my setting. I don't have lots of spare time to sit down and negotiate – even if it became a priority.'
Coach: 'This could mean that you are losing out on higher costs, lower profit margins, costly work practices which could be streamlined. Perhaps you should delegate negotiation tasks to colleagues – but do ensure that they are professionally trained first!'

7 'I tried to negotiate an initial deal recently but when it should have been implemented my "opponent" denied that we had set it up. What is the point?'
Coach: 'Wasn't there an agreed record of the meeting? Relying on memory and the "good nature" of the parties can be a big mistake – even when the parties have an established track record.'

Seven planning issues – more support from your coach

1 'I have heard it said that "failing to plan could really mean planning to fail!" Aren't top negotiators born, not made?'
Coach: 'The best negotiators are those who may appear to be negotiating off the cuff but you can be sure that, "off camera" they will have been: researching, making notes, checking track records, taking stock, assessing costs and/or market projections and preparing easily accessed notes for use in the meeting.'

2 'Why do some "authorities" recommend going to the other party's base for a meeting?'
Coach: 'There are no "rules" about where negotiations should be located. Skilled negotiators may have private preferences but, clearly, revealing them could prejudice the psychological comfort factors applying – and possibly the outcome, too!'

3 'I am most comfortable negotiating at my "home base". Why should I risk feeling uncomfortable by negotiating "away"?'
Coach: 'We can learn a lot about our "partners" or "opponents" when we see them in their own environments – and how they are viewed by their colleagues. This organization may become a significant "partner" for your organization – how well organized is it? How likely is it that their implementation of the deal you'll be making will be trouble-free, from what you have seen and heard?

4 'I always try to host meetings with other negotiators on "neutral territory". Is that a "better" idea?'
Coach: 'It can be if it is genuinely "neutral" and that there are no obvious distractions!'

5 'I am told that I tend to talk too much. Is that a disadvantage in negotiations? And how could I change it?'
Coach: 'If there are two people involved in the meeting, you should try not to talk for more than 50 per cent of the time! You could achieve that by trying to ask more questions and, when receiving questions, avoid *over*-answering.'

6 'People sometimes use anger when negotiating about a complaint. Is that acceptable behaviour?'
Coach: 'It is very important to practise self-control when negotiating! Discuss what has gone wrong objectively and calmly, and ask your contact what they can do to put things right. Never use personal insults or bad behaviour.'

7 'Why do some negotiators try to pretend they are something they are not?'
Coach: 'Some people may do this because they have low confidence or self-esteem. Let them see that reaching good deals is the best way of achieving a reputation as a trusted and effective negotiator.'

Seven powerful behaviours to practise in your next negotiation round

1 Don't start negotiating without preparing first (at least identifying the least and most desirable outcomes).

2 If misunderstandings should occur, check whether you could be to blame. If so, apologize, take personal steps to correct the position and ensure that it is not repeated.

3 Ask more questions – and listen carefully to the answers (seeking clarification when you are unsure what has been said/agreed). Do not close until your needs are satisfied.

4 Ensure that you build up and maintain your personal trust and integrity – for example by not withdrawing an offer made (especially when it has been accepted unambiguously).

5 Identify 'sticking points' carefully and encourage open discussion to find practical ways around them (or by balancing them with alternative concessions).

6 Practise summarizing and confirming actions to finalize a deal (ensuring that there are no errors and omissions which could lead to yet more negotiating later).

7 Don't dwell on 'might-have-beens' when negotiations have not been conclusive (or a 'cooling-off' period has elapsed without agreement). Set some new personal goals to continue this self-development process.

...And here's a bonus! Aspire to a higher-level understanding of the power of negotiating through this self-learning guide: Peter Fleming, *The Negotiation Coach* (John Murray Learning, 2015).

Answers

Through the week we have been challenging you to test your application of the principles described in each chapter. You can now summarize your results using the marking scales shown below.

Sunday:
1. a) 0 b) 1 c) 2 d) 0
2. a) 1 b) 0 c) 0 d) 2
3. a) 1 b) 0 c) 2 d) 0
4. a) 1 b) 2 c) 0 d) 0
5. a) 2 b) 0 c) 0 d) 1
6. a) 0 b) 0 c) 2 d) 1
7. a) 0 b) 0 c) 1 d) 2
8. a) 2 b) 0 c) 1 d) 0
9. a) 1 b) 2 c) 0 d) 0
10. a) 0 b) 2 c) 1 d) 1

Monday:
1. a) 1 b) 1 c) 1 d) 2
2. a) 0 b) 1 c) 2 d) 1
3. a) 0 b) 2 c) 1 d) 0
4. a) 1 b) 1 c) 1 d) 2
5. a) 1 b) 1 c) 1 d) 2
6. a) 1 b) 2 c) 0 d) 0
7. a) 0 b) 1 c) 2 d) 0
8. a) 2 b) 0 c) 1 d) 0
9. a) 0 b) 0 c) 2 d) 0
10. a) 1 b) 0 c) 2 d) 1

Tuesday:
1. a) 1 b) 1 c) 2 d) 3
2. a) 0 b) 0 c) 2 d) 1
3. a) 2 b) 0 c) 0 d) 0
4. a) 2 b) 0 c) 0 d) 1
5. a) 1 b) 2 c) 3 d) 1
6. a) 3 b) 1 c) 0 d) 0
7. a) 0 b) 2 c) 3 d) 0
8. a) 0 b) 0 c) 0 d) 2
9. a) 0 b) 2 c) 1 d) 3
10. a) 1 b) 0 c) 1 d) 2

Wednesday:
1. a) 2 b) 2 c) 0 d) 0
2. a) 0 b) 1 c) 0 d) 2
3. a) 1 b) 2 c) 0 d) 1
4. a) 2 b) 0 c) 1 d) 1
5. a) 0 b) 1 c) 2 d) 0
6. a) 1 b) 1 c) 2 d) 0
7. a) 0 b) 2 c) 1 d) 0
8. a) 1 b) 2 c) 0 d) 0
9. a) 2 b) 0 c) 1 d) 0
10. a) 1 b) 0 c) 2 d) 1

Thursday:
1. a) 0 b) 0 c) 2 d) 1
2. a) 0 b) 0 c) 1 d) 2
3. a) 0 b) 1 c) 1 d) 2
4. a) 2 b) 2 c) 0 d) 2
5. a) 1 b) 0 c) 2 d) 1
6. a) 2 b) 1 c) 1 d) 0
7. a) 2 b) 0 c) 0 d) 1
8. a) 0 b) 1 c) 2 d) 0
9. a) 1 b) 2 c) 0 d) 0
10. a) 1 b) 0 c) 0 d) 2

Friday:
1. a) 0 b) 0 c) 2 d) 1
2. a) 1 b) 2 c) 0 d) 0
3. a) 0 b) 0 c) 1 d) 2
4. a) 1 b) 0 c) 2 d) 0
5. a) 1 b) 2 c) 1 d) 0
6. a) 2 b) 3 c) 1 d) 1
7. a) 0 b) 2 c) 0 d) 1
8. a) 0 b) 0 c) 1 d) 2
9. a) 2 b) 0 c) 1 d) 0
10. a) 0 b) 2 c) 0 d) 1

Total score out of a possible 126: _____

Personal Action Plan

Objective	Target Date	Completed
1		
2		
3		
4		
5		

6		
7		
8		
9		
10		

ALSO AVAILABLE IN THE 'IN A WEEK' SERIES

For information about other titles
in the 'In A Week' series, please visit
www.teachyourself.co.uk